Fender Precision Basses
1951-1954

by Detlef Schmidt

CENTERSTREAM

Despite an exhaustive search, we have been unable to locate the publishers or copyright owners of some of the photos in this book. Therefore, we have proceeded on the assumption that no formal copyright claims have been filed on these works. If we have inadvertently published a previously copyrighted composition without permission, we advise the copyright owner(s) to contact us so that we may give credit in future editions.

This book is in no way intended to infringe on the intellectual property rights of any party. All products, brands, and names represented are trademarks or registered trademarks of their respective companies; information in this book was derived from the author's independent research and was not authorized, furnished or approved by other parties.

ISBN 978-1-57424-254-6
SAN 683-8022

P.O. Box 17878 Anaheim Hills, CA 92817
www.centerstream-usa.com

Layout and Design: Jürgen Wüst, Germany

CENTERSTREAM

Fender Precision Basses

1951-1954

by Detlef Schmidt

Table of Contents

Fender Precision Basses 1951-1954

Foreword by Preston Hubbard

I became aware of Fender basses in my early teens. Mid 60s. The shiny new P-basses and Jazz basses were way out of my price range, but I eventually could afford a new, red Mustang. In my late teens, I found a '66 Jazz Bass in a pawn shop for $75. The finish was stripped off, but the rest was all original. I loved that bass and had it for years, until it was stolen while I was on the road with the T-Birds.

The first time I really became aware of the original P-basses was when I met my friend, the late great Keith Ferguson. He had his '51, strung upside down for left hand playing. It was a beautiful chunk of wood, and was part of Keith's rumbling, signature sound. We called it the "motor boat". At the time, I was playing upright and my '66 with Roomful of Blues. Keith being a lefty, I never played his bass, but he always did. It was part of him, part of the Fergie persona and sound.

Years later, when I had replaced Keith in the T-Birds, Clifford Antone called me to his crib. He had a room full of vintage guitars and basses. He then presented me with my '52.

I was shocked, honored, and thankful! It was pristine, seemingly never touched. Brand new in the case (which still had the price tag on it). She became my favorite bass, replacing my '66 Jazz. There is no sound like the original P-basses. Just a slab of wood with a single pickup, but you can't beat it. There are some good copies and reissues out there now, but it just ain't the same. I've heard that Clifford, the patron saint of Austin blues, gave several other instruments to other players. He was like that. RIP, my dear friend Clifford!

I've played the '52 ever since, along with my main love, the upright. The '52 was lost for a few years when it was stolen and pawned by some junkies. Another dear friend, Gibby Haynes (Butthole Surfers) found it, bought it back, and kept it for me. He returned it to me in 2001. Love you, Gibby! The '52 has been all over the world with me, but lately I don't like flying her. Too risky. I've used my '52 on several records over the past years, and on most gigs. There is no sound, or feel, like those original basses.

When Detlef Schmidt initially contacted me about his book, I was thrilled and sent him several photos of the bass (#0256). Detlef put together a beautiful pre-production printing of the book and sent me one. I love it and show it to all my friends. Now the new and improved printing is coming out in the States. It is an important book to document the history of the original Fender basses. I am very excited about it!

Preston Hubbard
(March 2010)

Introduction

Leo Fender started producing the Precision bass sometime in 1951. There must be pre-production models before the start of serial production. In his book "Fender - The Sound Heard 'Round the World" Richard Smith reports, that Fender bought some tools needed for the production starting August 14th 1951. Most of the tools were bought in September 1951. This corresponds to the basses I have seen and documented, with the earliest one at the beginning of October 1951. Many details are unknown: how many basses were built, and what has become of them ?

In about 2002 I fell deeply in love with these first Fender bass guitars. I started collecting basses (thanks to Ebay) and acquiring photos of every bass I could. Most of the photos were send to me by fellow Precision Bass owners, and so were not made by professional photographers.

While searching the internet for more information I met a lot of beautiful people: Mike (who helped by adding his photo collection), George (with lots of theories and his article), Nacho (who wrote the Blackguard book and sent some nice e-mails), Dave (who owns 5 of 83), Prez (for sending me all the photos and giving me a good time in the 80s with his music), Erin (its good to see this bass in good hands), Sugarbeet (I got you infected), Roger from Canada (for giving me some good contacts and proof-reading) and Albert Molinaro (who always had time for discussions).

Thanks to Ken and Clive for sending their pictures and having good discussions, Joe from Axeactely Music and Roland from "Bass Professor". I am sure I have forgotten somebody. If so, my apologies - you know who you are!

This book would not have been possible without the Fender Discussion Page and all the information and help of its members.

Detlef Schmidt
(March 2010)

A History of the Development and Early Production of the Fender Precision Bass

By: George P. Edmonston Jr.

Any discussion of the history of the Fender Precision bass must begin with its creator, Clarence Leo Fender, and it's important to say right up top that Leo Fender did not "invent" the electric bass. By the time he was developing and manufacturing musical instruments and amplifiers in the 1940s, the groundwork for a louder, smaller bass instrument was already well-established.

What he did do was nothing less than create and manufacture the world's first production-line electric bass, in a package that was affordable, portable, practical, easily playable and recordable, and that someone with minimal skills could adjust and repair. The sound of the Fender bass came to dominate the bottom-end in virtually every genre of popular music, and music has never been the same. Finally, here was a bass instrument that looked good enough and sounded good enough to withstand the snobbery and contempt of the upright bass player, although the rivalry in the beginning was serious and intense.

Beginning in the 1920s, Lloyd Loar, Gibson's legendary luthier, had developed an experimental "electrified" upright bass. However, the instrument was never sold to the public. Pictures show something resembling the "stick" basses made today. It was all peghead (traditional URB scroll design), neck, fingerboard and pickup.

In the mid-1930s, George Beauchamp's Electro String company produced for Rickenbacher a similar-looking electric bass instrument, which measured 58-inches long by 6-inches at its widest point.

In February 1935, Seattle music teacher and radio personality Paul Tutmarc introduced the Audiovox, considered by many historians to be the first fretted bass in history.

By 1938, another manufacturer, the Regal Company, had its own answer to Loar, Beauchamp and Tutmarc.

Leo was aware of these early basses, was clearly influenced by them, and also knew of the moderate success Gibson had enjoyed for several decades with its "Mando Bass," an instrument resembling a giant mandolin and featuring a fretted neck for the precise fingering of notes.

In 1945, he began experimenting with his own version of a pickup that would reproduce deep music. Naming his device the "Direct String Pickup," Leo actually placed a few ads in newspapers announcing the availability of the new electronic and promising its adaptability to the upright bass.

Leo's approach to electrifying the bottom end now began to change, as he worked to try and adapt his new pickup to something resembling an oversized guitar. This is the beginning of the Precision bass. His vision partly came from local musicians impacted after World War II by the downsizing of the "Big Band" to smaller units, where volume and player mobility were becoming of paramount importance. Leo was a good listener and words like "smaller" and "fretted" began to show up in his discussions.

Leo Fender was born on Aug. 10, 1909, in a hay barn located between Anaheim and Fullerton in southern California. His father was a truck farmer, his mother a homemaker. Except for three years during the Depression, in which he worked for the California Highway Department in San Luis Obispo, Leo spent his life living and working in and around Fullerton. He held an associate's degree from a junior college in accounting. He married at 25 and started his own business at 28. He was blind in one eye, loved to tinker, was a ham radio operator and a workaholic. He played saxophone in his high school band, but never learned to play guitar.

Dale Hyatt standing in front of the Fender Radio Repair Shop (1948)

Drawing on a long-standing interest in electronics, specifically radios and public address systems, Leo said goodbye to state employment in 1938, and moved back home. He opened a small electronics shop... Fender's Radio Service... in rented space at a Golden Eagle service station located at the corner of Spadra Blvd. and Santa Fe near downtown Fullerton. Today, Spadra is known as Harbor Blvd., still one of the main thoroughfares running north and south in the city. His phone number was "6," no area code. In addition to repairing radios, he also built and rented PA equipment, and sold phonographic records and sheet music.

Among his many customers were musicians needing repairs on their amps. Business growth soon demanded more space, so he moved from the service station to an address a few doors away...112 Spadra. Here he would meet Doc Kauffman, a local violinist. The two would form a partnership for the development and manufacture of amplifiers and lap steel guitars to take advantage of the Hawaiian music craze brought back to the states by military personnel who had served in the Pacific Theater during World War II.

They also combined their talents to produce a dependable phonographic record changer (eventually sold to RCA for $5,000) and to experiment with an electronic guitar pickup which allowed the strings to pass through and not over the top of the wound magnetic wire coil. The year was 1943. Their company was known as the Kauffman & Fender Manufacturing Corp., or "K&F" for short.

By 1945 more space was needed. Doc and Leo moved again, this time to 107 S. Spadra. Soon after, Leo also made the

First two metal buildings on Pomona St. in Fullerton, CA, where the Fender Co. started

decision to get out of radio repair work and dedicate his efforts to musical instruments and equipment. His workaholic lifestyle began to take its toll on Doc. In 1946, the one-time violinist gave his notice, sold his interest in the company to his partner, and said goodbye to K&F.

Now the sole owner, Leo changed the name of the company to the Fender Manufacturing Company. In the spring of 1946, he was still working and using his radio shop as a lab and assembly area. He also had a small shed out back. Needing more space, he built another small shed a block to the north, on the alley between Commonwealth and Amerige Avenues.

In May 1946, he decided to make the move toward a real manufacturing facility and relocated to two small corrugated tin buildings he had built at the corner of Santa Fe and Ponoma Avenues. Each was 30x60 feet in size, with no heat and no place to use the bathroom. They were erected by the California Construction Steel Company of Los Angeles and passed final inspection in December. The building to the west was the metal shop and assembly area; the one to the east was the wood shop. A nearby garage with dirt floors was used for storage. Radio-Tel, a major radio and electronic parts wholesaler, was responsible for selling and distributing Fender's products. It is at this legendary address that Leo Fender would develop and manufacture the first Broadcaster, Esquire, Telecaster and "No" Caster electric guitars.

The new brick building (1952)

Photographs of the property show the buildings next to a vacant lot immediately to the west and extending to the corner of Pomona Ave. Here, in 1950, Leo built a double-roofed cinder block building. It included something company employees had long needed. Now they wouldn't have to cross the street to the train station to use the rest rooms.

In these three small buildings, the two tin ones and the cinder block, Leo developed, prototyped and manufactured the first Fender

p. 287 of Richard Smith's book, Fender: The Sound Heard 'Round the World) account for 83 basses. Was this the total number made? Or only the number shipped, while others waited in storage for delivery in 1952? No one knows for sure. Because the company was tiny, with no storage space for anything other than

Fender Christmas Party (1950)

Precision basses.

Serious work on a prototype began in 1950 and instruments were finally ready for shipping by the end of October, 1951. No one knows how many prototypes were made because none has survived. Collectors have debated for years about exactly when the first production-run basses finally left the factory for retail, but it was certainly not before October 31 and no later than late November.

However, we do have a better idea of how many '51 P-basses were made. Leo's personal notes from that year (faithfully reproduced on

materials in production, my personal belief is that the number 83 represents the total of all the basses made.

Also from Leo's notes (and Smith's book), a proposed schedule for the first six months of 1952 show the company planned to build 400 basses. It is not known if this quota was ever achieved.

Approximately 20 employees worked for Fender at this time, many of them Mexican-Americans. In 1952, the number would grow to about 28. Several of these...Lupe Lopez, Tadeo Gomez and Lydia "Lillie" Sanchez...

have become legends among collectors of early Fenders. Lupe and Lydia did electronic assembly, while Tadeo, probably the company's first master craftsman, cut bodies and hand-shaped necks. Gomez worked at Fender from the late 1940s to around 1957, when he left Fender because of a supposed fallout with management. He went to work in construction for Disneyland until the mid-1960s. Returning to Fender, now owned by CBS, he took a position as a maintenance man. It boggles the mind to think that a man of such talents as he had demonstrated during his first tenure with the company would now be reduced to pushing a broom. Born Jaurga Tadeo Gomez in Jalisco, Mexico in 1902, he lived in La Habra, Calif., while working at Fender and Disneyland. He passed away on November 25, 1986 at age 83.

Tadeo Gomez initials

His name or initials penciled to the butt-end of early Fender necks, also the neck pockets of many bodies, are highly prized. An authentic Gomez signature can appear in different ways, from blocked letters to script to first name spelled out. However, block-shaped "TG" is the

Serial numbers stamped on the bridge plate

most common. There are also rare examples of Tadeo necks in which only the date appears. Company policy called for dating to use a MMDDYY format, with the numbers separated by either slashes or dashes.

Penciled neck and body dates remain the best way to date an old Precision. Unfortunately, serial numbers, which appear stamped on the bridge plate on the pickup side of the saddles (neck plates are blank), are virtually useless for fine-tuning the day or week an instrument rolled off the assembly line because they were issued with no consideration given to sequencing the numbers

As an example, Vol. 22 of *Werner's List: The Directorate of Tube Alloys*, a must-have for Fender collectors because it remains the best of the hard-copy lists of Fender serial numbers covering the years 1950s-1990s, shows serial number 0009 for a May 1952 bass, while 0064 was given to a 1/28/52 P-bass. Most serial numbers on Fender's earliest basses are of the four-digit variety, with zeros included as digits, but Werner also documents rare three-

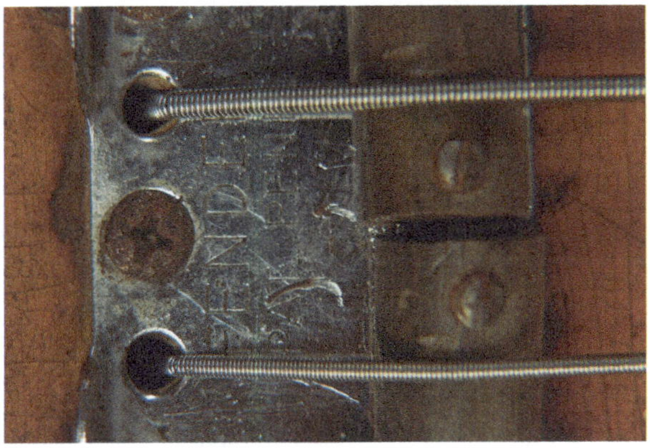

Phillips screws on bridge plate

digit and very rare two digit serials. Three-digit serials appear as late as 1953. It is also possible for a guitar and bass to have the same serial. Regardless of how many numbers make up the serial, it is also normal for one of the numbers to be slightly off-line from the others. (Potentiometers provide other aids to dating which we will discuss shortly.)

As well, screws can also help with dating. Basses issued in 1951 and 1952 tend to have slotted screws for pickguards, necks, control

Masking tape date "Mary"

Slot screws on tuners

plates, tuners, saddles and to help raise and lower pickups. However, bridges are often attached to bodies with Phillips, and this leads to the point that it is possible to find these early Precisions with a mix of original slotted and Phillips screws. In general, slotted means earlier, Phillips later.

Other initials and names found on basses (and guitars) from this period include "CD" for Charlie Davis, "TK," "Bill," and "Eddie" or "EM" for Eddie Miller or Mendoza. The presence of masking tape dates on the inside of pickup and control cavities is also standard, and the names Gloria, Virginia, Mary and Eleanor are common. These ladies were responsible for harness assembly and installation work.

"D"-stamp

In addition to initials, names and dates, a mysterious "D" stamp is generally found on most if not all Fender necks and bodies made between 1951 and 1954. Beginning in 1953, the stamp is less frequent. In rare cases, the "D" can be hand-written. No one has yet produced a plausible explanation for these stamps, but their appearance is a good sign a neck or body is authentic.

Body and neck dates only signify when components were finished and ready for spraying. They should never be used to fine-tune the dating of a bass or guitar because necks and bodies often sat around for weeks or sometimes months before they were pulled off the rack to make an instrument.

As Smith tells it, Leo left a fairly extensive paper trail from 1951 that helps trace the development of the Precision bass. What they show is that production of necks and bodies could not have started until mid-August because that's when Leo purchased the tools necessary to put the instrument into full production. For example, on Aug. 14 he took receipt for the die that would trim bass keys; on Aug. 28 the saw arbor (mandrell) for the neck; Sept. 1, the template for necks; Sept. 13 the template for bodies.

Designed to resemble an "oversized Telecaster," a fact Leo would always deny, the first Precision bodies were, like their guitar counterparts, made of two pieces of ash, were matched and laminated to resemble a single piece of wood (one-piece and three-piece bodies do exist but are rare), and were painted with a see-through blonde finish. It is also true that on some of his earliest guitars Fender used pine, but pine, as far as historians are aware, was never used to make basses.

Ash was not a tone-wood decision. To Leo and his staff, the popular hardwood simply looked better than other woods beneath the '50s fashionable blonde color. Also, weight was not taken into account.

Bodies started as 14x21x2-inch blanks and were cut and shaped using pin routers. They cost $7.47 each to make. The first basses have no body contours, only squared-off cutaways, and are often referred to as "planks." Contours on bass bodies appear after the introduction of the Fender Stratocaster in mid-1954.

Necks were cut from 4x33-inch maple blanks on a 34-inch scale. The length was derived from a physics textbook borrowed from Fender secretary Elizabeth Nagel Hayzlett, a student at UCLA. Always practical, Leo determined the length as the longest players could easily fret. He saw no use in making an instrument, bassists would find uncomfortable

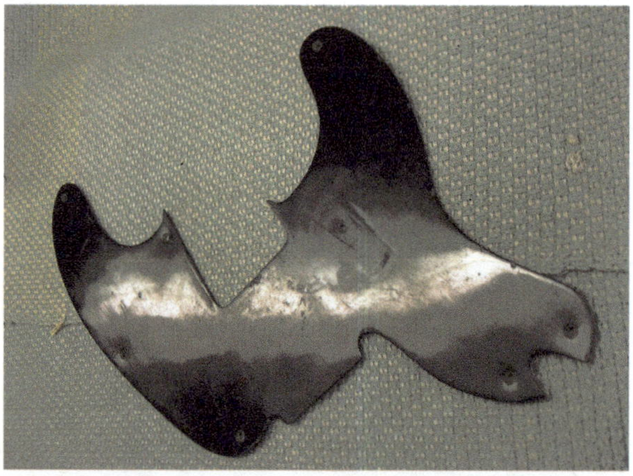

Pickguard

to play, deeming it marketing suicide.

Regarding the "baseball bat" image these early necks have, my experience has been that, as a group, they are anything but. Although rounded and chunky in feel and appearance, plank necks are quite comfortable to play, even among players who have smaller hands and fingers. Because the concept of neck widths labeled as "A" (1 ½-inches at the nut), "B" (1 5/8-inches) or "C" (1 ¾-inches) was still many years in the future (circa 1960), it is

Milky-white to butterscotch

not possible to label early bass necks in these terms. However, for purposes of comparing an early neck with a 1960s neck, at the nut, a 1951-52 neck tends to be slightly less than a C-width. Because they were hand-finished, they are all subtly different and resist language that attempts to group them together in a monolithic block.

Early planks feature a black pickguard cut from 4x8-foot sheets of 1/16-inch phenolic plastic material collectors sometimes refer to as "bakelite." To give them a shiny appearance, the top surface was generally coated with a clear lacquer finish. Over time, environmental stresses on phenolic plastic play havoc and so many of the earliest pickguards have not survived to the present, having blistered and disintegrated many years ago.

Today, the "butterscotch" look of many early bodies with original paint has given rise to the idea that Fender offered two different finishes. Not so. Fender in the early 50s never offered anything other than see-through blonde for its basses. When freshly painted, the appearance was generally milky-white and thin enough to allow the grain of the wood to peak through. Exposure to light and tobacco smoke, among other things, caused the clear lacquer finish on top of the white paint (top coat) to turn yellow, then butterscotch, depending on levels of exposure and age. Instruments in which the top coat was not applied retained their milky-white appearance longer. It's interesting to note that some eyewitness accounts from the early 50s, along with scanty photo evidence, tell of seeing Esquires and Telecasters finished in black. However, there seems to be no evidence to suggest this was ever done with the Precision.

A "thumbrest" or "tugbar" below the G-string and mounted on the pickguard just

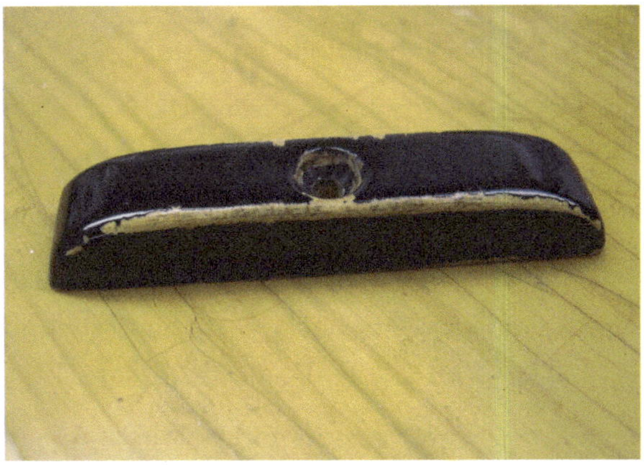

behind the lower horn, was a part of the design, and most of the earliest Precisions feature this appointment, but a rare few do not. The earliest

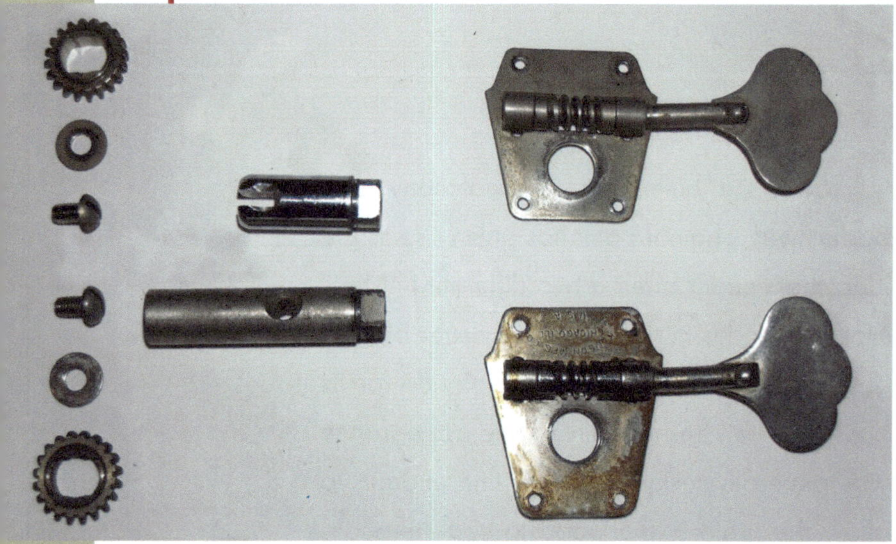

Fender used modified Kluson upright bass tuners

ones are made of wood and painted black, although some unpainted examples exist. Tugs were attached to bodies with a single screw, although Smith's book has pictured (p. 104) a very early plank with a two-screw thumbrest, a feature that would not become regular production until 1957.

The first tuners were bought from the Kluson Company of Chicago and were upright bass tuners cut to size to fit the new Fender bass. String posts were custom-made at Fender. Tuners were attached to headstocks with slotted screws; bolts used to attach flywheels to the tuner assembly were also slotted, and the plates to which everything was attached did not fit snug against the headstock.

Fret wire was nickel-silver in composition and installed from the side on slots sawn after the position markers had been drilled and dots affixed. Once frets, nut and truss rod were installed, the neck was hand-sanded and sprayed with clear lacquer. After the neck cured, frets were dressed and polished.

Basses made in 1951 have truss rods with slotted adjustment screws, a characteristic that gradually disappears in early 1952, as the rods begin to feature two separate slots placed at 90 degrees of each other. However, some 1952 and a few 1953 basses feature slotted. Rod screws were machined, cut and threaded at Fender.

Bridge, control and neck plates were also done in-house. The material was chrome-plated steel made from Col Rolled sheet steel. For years, a company called Cal-Tron Plating did all the chrome and gold plating for Fender.

Also, Fender made its own strap buttons

Different jack cups

and both guitars and basses used the same buttons. Bridge saddles came from a phenolic material just like that of the pickguards.

Jack cups were of two varieties: The first ones were machined in-house from B1113 steel material and chrome-plated. The unit was pressed into the wood and had a tendency over time to work itself loose. On these, at least three different knurl versions have been identified. In late 52, Fender switched to a jack

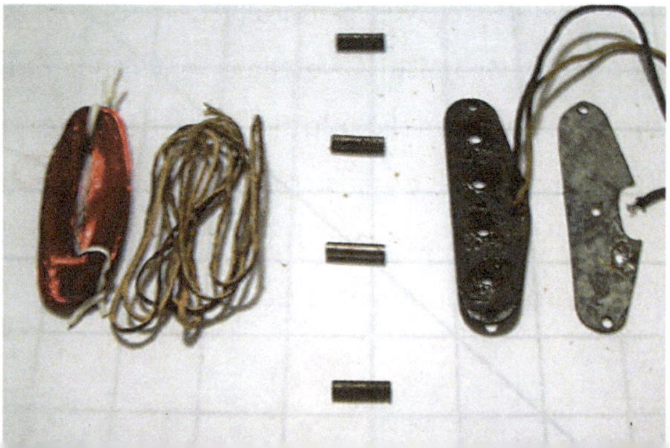

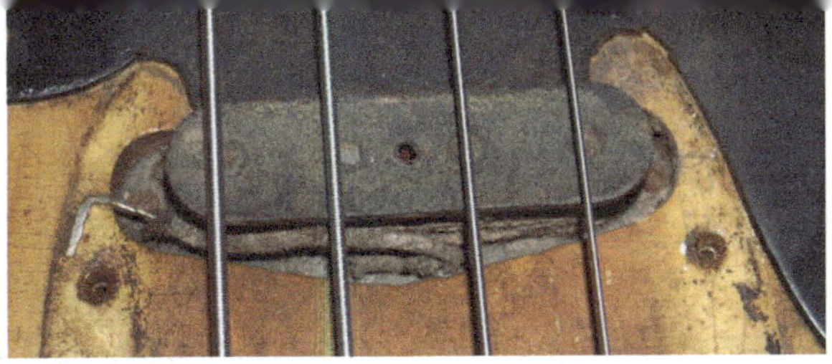

The first pickups had all poles flat, then the A and D pole were raised. Looks like this change was made somewhere in 1952 already. The pickup was put in wax (making the twine black) or just left without wax.

cup made of pressed steel that was held in place with an anchor plate.

Steel-wrapped gut strings were used to test early bass prototypes. Later, Fender strings were supplied by the V.C. Squire Company of Battle Creek, Michigan.

Fender made its own pickup fiber plates and bodies on punch presses, with dies Leo designed from the early days and sourced from tool and die supplier, Race & Olmstead. Arnold Engineering and the Permanent Magnet Company of Indiana supplied the magnets, which were sand-cast Alnico V magnets. Each pickup housed four magnets, or poles, which in 1951 were mostly flush across the top fiber. By 1952, staggered poles begin to appear.

Fender single-coil bass pickups from the 1950s feature top and bottom flatwork made of a fiber material which is always black in color. Telecaster basses of the late 1960s have pickups featuring this same material, but the color is gray. Pickups from both eras show a distinctive hole in the middle of the flatwork, there to anchor the pickup while winding was in progress. All Fender bass pickups were hand wound until the CBS takeover in 1965.

In the assembly process, a blonde twine was wound around the pickup wiring, the twine hiding the wire from view. Once done, the pickup was then dipped in black wax, giving the blonde twine the expected black, waxy appearance, although some early pickups were not dipped and still show the blonde twine. Beware: It is also true many pickups sporting blonde twine have been rewound. With these examples, the twine material often looks too clean and new to be very old.

For potentiometers, Fender used off-the-shelf, readily available components made by Stackpole, Clarostat or Chicago Telephone Service (CTS). The rating for both volume and tone pots was 250K. More often than not, Clarostats were used in 1951-52. These pots are easy to spot and feature a black or blue ink print with a CM number, plus a 140XXX code for manufacturer. The fourth digit is the year and the fifth and six digits represent the week. Example, 140215 would be a Clarostat pot made in 1952, the 15th week.

Stackpole pots show a 304XXX manufacturer code, with the fourth digit the year and the fifth and six digits the week. Example, 304127 would be a Stackpole pot made the 27th week of 1951.

Clarostat pot

1951 PRECISION BASS

The very first Precision Basses, produced in late 1951, were wired as illustrated in these diagrams. Although Leo didn't seem to like using Astron brand caps in the professional model guitars, he did have plenty on hand for use in the amplifiers, so they were used in the P-Bass until the first shipment of Cornell-Dubilier .1mfd "Chiclets" arrived. These early bass guitars also featured a resistor,* most likely intended to protect the cones in amplifiers that were unprepared for that famous, deep, P-Bass thump.

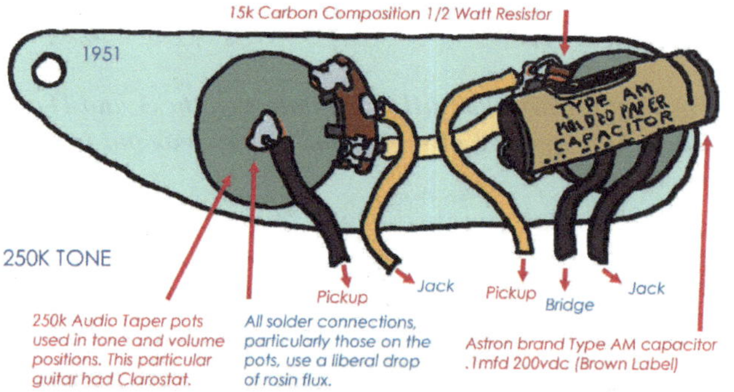

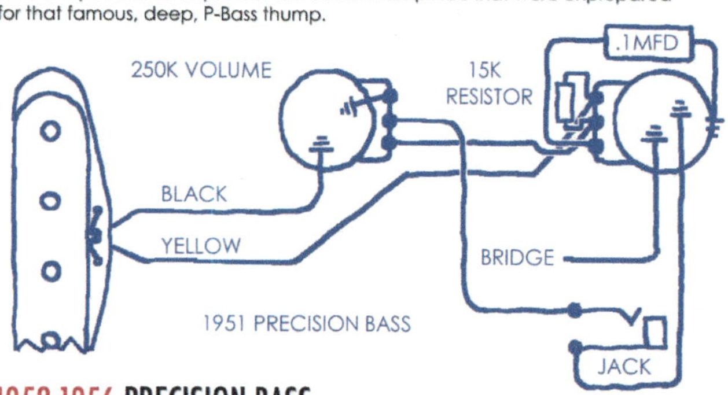

1955 Precision Bass

1952-1956 PRECISION BASS

After the first few months of production, the wiring was changed slightly in the Precision Bass, as illustrated here. Notably, the Astron capacitor was replaced with a Cornell-Dubilier brand .1mfd 150vdc "Chiclet." Every Precision released between 1952 and 1956 will use this same brown, wax covered cap. As with all Fender products of the 1950s, the wiring is cloth-covered and the pots are generally Stackpole brand 250k audio taper. Output jacks come from Switchcraft and the control plates were stamped in-house.

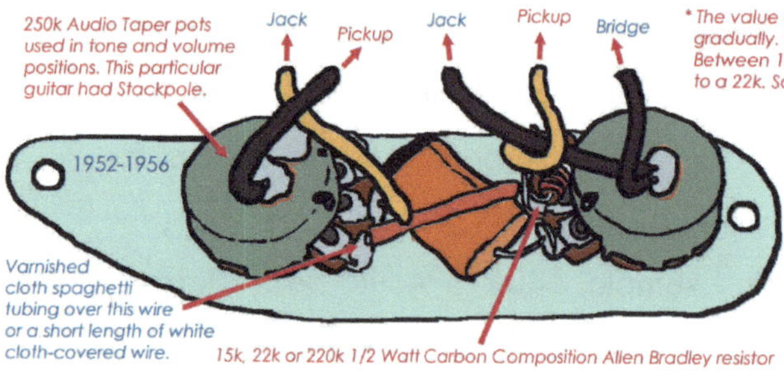

* The value of the resistor was raised gradually. 1951-52 models have a 15k. Between 1952 and 1955 this changed to a 22k. Some late basses have a 220k.

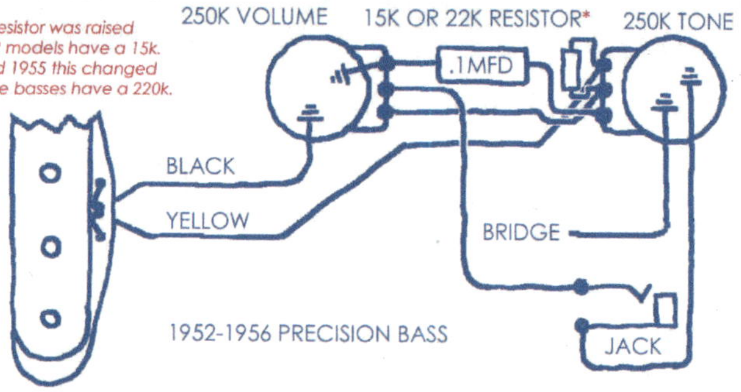

1956-1957 PRECISION BASS

Here we see the hot wire from the pickup move to the volume pot and the resistor is dropped altogether.

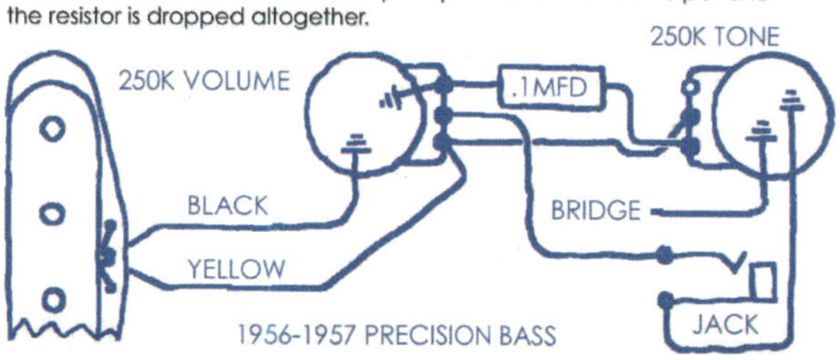

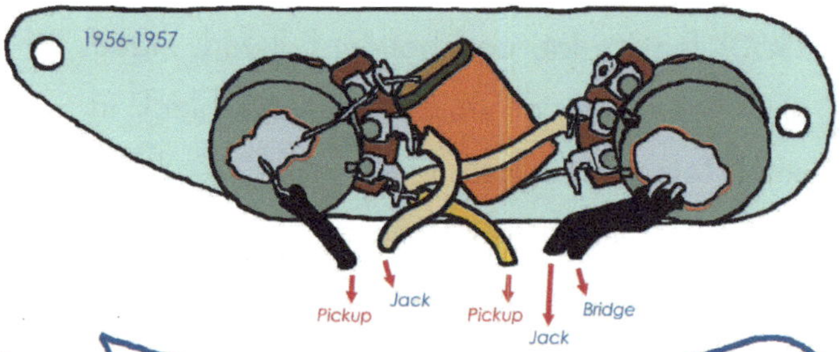

1957-1961 PRECISION BASS

In 1957 the Precision was given a complete overhaul and the new "Split P" pickups were introduced. Three types of C-D wax capacitors were used during the 5 year period before the introduction of ceramic caps. Pots are generally Stackpole.

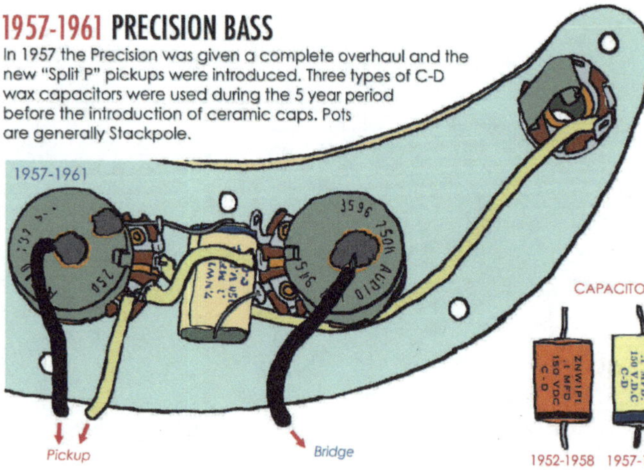

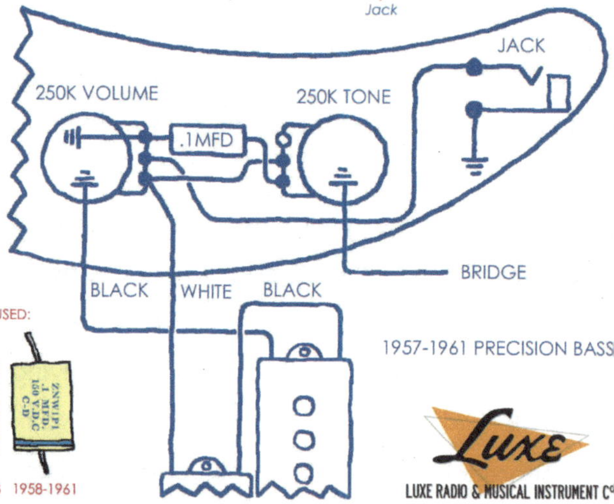

CAPACITORS USED:

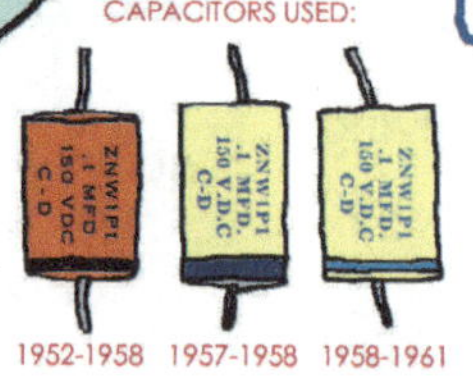

LUXE RADIO & MUSICAL INSTRUMENT Cº

Wiring diagram used by friendly permission of Donovan from Luxeradio.com

Different water-slide decals

The same pattern works also for CTS and its 137XXX manufacturer code. Example, 137348 would be a CTS pot made in 1953, the 48th week.

Early planks also featured wax paper-covered foil capacitors made by Astron or Cornell-Dublier. Both had a rating of .1 MFD. The very earliest 51 P-basses feature the tubular-shaped Astron brand, which were phased out when the Cornell-Dubliers arrived because Leo felt the Astrons lacked the quality necessary for installation in a professional model instrument. Affectionately known as "Chiclets," the C-Ds are brownish in color.

Fender used cloth wiring colored black and yellow (brown when aged) to connect all electronic components.

Fender bought its water-slide decals from companies like Safe-T-Gal of Santa Ana, Calif., and also from Associated Silk Screen. The cloud shape of an early '50s P-bass decal--the halo affect the adhesive backing gives off in certain light--is fairly expansive and does not follow the shapes of the individual letters as we often see in later decals.

For years, Fender bought its bone nut material from Winterbottom, Samuel & Sons from Egg Harbor City, New Jersey. Necks

Original cases are hard to find

Rounding out the harness was a 15K (sometimes a 22K) half-watt carbon composition resistor made by the Allen-Bradley company.

were slotted and then the nut installed prior to lacquering. Cutting and setting up the nut was done by hand and could take up to 30 minutes

Plastic-leather gig bags

to complete.

Cases came from the Bulwin Manufacturing Company of Costa Mesa, Calif. The earliest cases, issued from 1951-53, are shaped like a guitar and are known as "thermometer" cases. Many original examples of these for six-string guitars have survived, but it is unclear if any were ever issued for bass, as no one contacted in researching this story could ever recall seeing one. Fender did offer brown-colored, plastic-leather gig bags as a protection for the Precision bass. Examples in good condition today are rare. In 1953, Fender switched to the "poodle" case, so named because of the poodle appearance of the felt material used to line the interior. Tweed was introduced in 1954, manufactured by the Victoria Luggage Company.

More about screws, Fender sourced wood screws, machine screws and set screws from a company called Mahl Steel in Huntington Park, Calif. They were nickel-plated but not heat-treated. Old screws are easy to spot, as they are only threaded three-quarters of the way up the shaft. On early '50s basses, this applies to virtually every screw, regardless of size.

Playing an early 1950s Fender Precision bass is holding history in your hands. The pickup sounds distinctive and delivers that fundamental Fender Precision tone that has been world famous for over 50 years, with amazing cut-through-the-mix and beautiful mids. It's the sound, along with the instrument, that launched a revolution in American popular music.

Sources:

Bacon, Tony; Day Paul: The Fender Book: A complete history of Fender electric guitars. San Francisco, Calif.: GPI Books, Miller Freeman, Inc., 1992.

Bacon, Tony; Moorhouse, Barry. The Bass Book: A complete illustrated history of bass guitars. GPI Books, Miller Freeman, Inc. 1995

Banos, Nacho. The Blackguard: A detailed history of the early Fender Telecaster years 1950-1954. Published by Ignacio Banos and Nacho Banos, 2005.

Black, J.W.; Molinaro, Albert. The Fender Bass: An Illustrated History. Milwaukee, Wisc.: Hal Leonard Corporation, 2001.

Blasquiz, Klaus. The Fender Bass. Hal Leonard Publishing, 1990.

Brosnac, Donald (ed.). Guitar History: Volume #1. San Francisco, Calif.: Paul C's Guitar Products, 1983.

Duchossoir, A.R. Guitar Identification: How to date the guitars made by Fender-Gibson-Gretsch-Martin. New Revised and Enlarged Edition. Hal Leonard Publishing, 1983.
Fender Discussion Page, 1999-2009.
www.fenderforum.com

Fender Precision bass, serial number 0064, TG neck dated 1/28/52.

Fullerton, George. Guitar Legends: The Evolution of the Guitar from Fender to G&L. Fullerton, Calif.: Centerstream Publishing, 1993.

Harris, Norm; Swartz, David. Norman's Rare Guitars. Los Angeles, Calif.: Swartz Publishing Inc., 1999.

Roberts, Jim. How the Fender Bass Changed the World. Hal Leonard Publishing, 2001.

Smith, Richard R. Fender: The Sound 'Heard Round the World. Fullerton, Calif.: Garfish Publishing Company, 1995.

Vintage Guitar Info Guy. Vintage Fender Guitars, Basses, Amps. Model Information (popular website). www.provide.net/~cfh/fender2.html

Werner, James. Werner's List: The Directorate of Tube Alloys, Vol. 22. Wapello, Iowa: Louisa Publishing Co. Ltd., 1998.

Wheeler, Tom. American Guitars: An Illustrated History. New York: Harper & Row, 1982.

White, Forrest. Fender: The Inside Story. GPI Books, Miller Freeman, Inc., 1994.

Two variations of inside cloth color

Theories about Production Numbers

Theory 1 - Based on serial numbers:

This is a list of serial numbers that I put together a while ago with the help of the James Werner list as well as the help of George and Bill. It has 219 basses listed. The James Werner list is known for listing numbers without seeing the instruments, so I doubt that the numbers #1632 and #1897, that he lists, were stamped on a bridge. My believe is that serial numbers on early plank basses, that were stamped on bridges, go from 0001 until 1499. In the years of my research I have never seen any number higher than #1493.

As you can see there is no direct correlation between serial number and date of manufacture. The bridges must have been in a box or in a few boxes. The only thing you can say is, that in 1951 they used numbers beginning 0001 and 0100 and 0300, in 1952 the 0200 numbers were common, in 1955 the 0500, 0600 are likely. No number higher than 0500 seems to have been used in 1951. Nothing else.

Out of these instruments, 42 were made in later 1954, 1955 or 1956. If the production was changed to contours in the middle of 1954, this would mean, that these instruments are not slab body basses. This totals 42 out of 219 instruments. This is about 20 %. When 20 % is taken from 1500 bridges with serial numbers, it equals about 300 basses. This means about 1200 slab body basses exist.

The problem with this theory is, that Werner lists also basses with only 2 digits or 3 digits as serial number. Maybe they were reported wrong, e.g. #0042 was reported as #42.

Then a friend showed me pictures of his bass #127, no "0" was stamped on it. This is the only example of a 3 digit serial number I have ever seen, but its for sure that they exist. #619 is the highest number that Werner lists with 3 digits.

Leo Fender (1949)

0005	
0008	Mar 52
0009	May 52
0011	Dec 51
0015	Jan 52
0028	Jul 52
0033	
0036	Nov 51
0037	
0038	Apr 52
0042	51
0043	Oct 51
0052	Jul 52
0058	Jan 52
0060	Apr 52
0064	Jan 52
0072	
0079	
0082	
0107	Mar 52
0113	
0115	
0118	Sep 52
0127	Oct 51
0128	
0135	
0138	52
0153	52
0154	Jun 52
0160	Jun 52
0161	Oct 51
0163	Oct 51
0166	Jul 52
0171	
0177	
0178	
0185	
0187	
0212	Nov 51
0214	Feb 52
0215	Jul 52
0220	Feb 52
0221	52
0225	Feb 52
0238	Apr 52
0239	Jan 52
0241	51
0245	Apr 52
0248	Mar 53
0256	52
0262	Sep 52
0263	
0264	Dec 51
0272	Jan 52
0274	52
0281	
0284	Jul 52
0287	Apr 52
0289	52
0299	52
0313	52
0326	
0327	Dec 51
0329	Jul 52
0335	Jun 52
0357	Jun 52
0362	Oct 53
0368	Dec 51
0370	
0382	Dec 51
0384	Jun 52
0385	51
0386	Nov 51
0388	Apr 52
0396	Mar 52
0409	
0410	52
0427	Mar 52
0432	Nov 51
0436	Nov 51
0437	Nov 51
0442	Sep 52
0444	Sep 52
0452	52
0457	Jan 52
0466	Sep 52
0469	Jul 54
0470	Nov 51
0475	54
0482	
0484	
0507	Mar 52
0517	Aug 55
0521	Mar 54
0533	May 52
0534	Jul 55
0550	55
0557	Nov 52
0563	52
0571	
0573	Nov 52
0579	Jul 55
0585	Mar 55
0590	
0592	52
0608	Nov 54
0619	
0623	Jan 53
0624	Jan 55
0642	Jan 55
0648	Apr 55
0667	53
0669	55
0672	Feb 53
0674	52
0676	
0685	Sep 53
0691	Nov 53
0710	55
0730	May 54
0735	
0738	Dec 52
0739	
0743	May 55
0747	
0749	53
0761	Jul 53
0763	Dec 53
0767	Jul 54
0772	53
0786	Apr 55
0788	Dec 54
0795	Sep 53
0796	52
0799	53
0804	Aug 53
0819	Apr 57
0821	Feb 53
0822	
0832	Apr 55
0834	May 53
0836	Dec 52
0840	Nov 53
0848	Sep 54
0849	Feb 52
0852	Mar 55
0854	Mar 55
0856	Apr 53
0863	Mar 53
0870	Apr 55
0875	
0876	53
0879	54
0881	Jul 53
0917	53
0924	
0929	Feb 55
0936	Jul 53
0948	53
0959	
0968	Oct 53
0975	Jul 53
0999	54
1001	
1021	55
1023	55
1025	53
1026	
1032	53
1034	
1056	Oct 53
1070	
1074	
1086	
1088	Jul 53
1093	54
1118	
1119	53
1139	Mar 55
1150	Jul 54
1167	Jan 53
1169	54
1176	
1179	55
1190	Jul 54
1204	Oct 54
1208	Nov 54
1212	Feb 52
1226	54
1228	Nov 54
1230	Sep 53
1250	53
1264	Jul 55
1267	Oct 53
1272	54
1275	Nov 54
1284	Jun56
1301	Mar 53
1311	Dec 52
1314	
1321	Oct 53
1331	53
1332	Aug 55
1341	Jun 56
1351	52
1368	May 53
1374	
1377	
1382	Jul 53
1386	May 53
1394	Jul 54
1406	Dec 52
1407	53
1409	Mar 55
1415	
1430	Mar 55
1433	Jul 54
1440	
1443	53
1493	

Theory 2 - Based on decal numbers:

In a 1951 inventory that Nacho Banos found in the archives of Richard Smith, Fender lists 453 bass bridge covers, 406 bass pickup covers, 656 bass string ferrules and 924 bass decals. In his book, Richard Smith reports, that 83 basses were sold in 1951. This leads to the assumption that about 1000 decals were ordered, give or take a few. Now if some of these beginning decals (easy to recognize by the shape of their cloud) are found on 1955 or later basses, this means that about 1000 slab body basses do exist.

But at the end of 1953, it seems that Fender did order the new decals with the cloud closer to the letters. They are to be found on later 53 basses, as well as the earlier decals are to be found on basses as late as 1955. So there is an overlapping of those decals.

Theory 3 - Based on estimated production planning:

In his book, Richard Smith writes about estimated production planning for the first half of 1952 and mentions 400 Precision Basses and 400 Bassman amps. Taking this estimation as true, this would mean 800 basses in '52, 800 basses in '53, 400 basses in '54 (until they changed to the contoured model) and the 83 basses that were sold in '51. This leads to an estimated number of about 2000 basses. But its more than likely that the sales estimations were too high.

This is one of the first Precision Bass instruments. The photo was made by Leo Fender. Maybe a prototype, note the missing word "Precision Bass" on the decal and the two screws in the tugbar.

Wiring benches

Bob Hines working in the metal shop on Pomona Ave. (1952)

#0171

Keith Ferguson

Keith Ferguson is the first bass player I ever saw playing a Slab Body Precision Bass. It looked more than cool. To me the first Fabulous Thunderbirds records are still among my favourite blues records. Some years ago, I wanted to know what happened to Keith Ferguson. I was sad to find out that he was already dead, having passed away April 29, 1997. He played with the Fabulous Thunderbirds from their formation until some time in the mid 1980's, when he was replaced by Preston Hubbard. His later bands were the Tail Gators and the Solid Senders. The Solid Senders CD is a good album with the bass mixed right to the front. At this time Ferguson had already sold his 52 P-Bass.

Here is a part of an article about Keith. It was published shortly before the death of Keith Ferguson.

Beautiful Loser
Keith Ferguson: No Apologies, No Regrets

(by Josh Alan Friedman, "Tell the truth until they bleed", Backbeat Books, used by friendly permission)

"I have to admit, there's a guaranteed future in dirty dishes, which there ain't in blues," concedes Keith Ferguson. "I seem to be the only one who regards himself as a professional musician. Our lead singer's a dishwasher in the back of some restaurant. If he put half the energy into booking our band that he puts into scrubbin' dishes, we'd be fartin' through silk. But he'd rather do dishes."

Ferguson, Austin's once-reigning blues bassist and ultimate hipster, is out to pasture. His pasture is a rustic wooded estate in the hills below downtown Austin. His voice is a dead ringer for that of William Holden narrating Sunset Boulevard. Some wonder whether Ferguson's fall from grace was conspiratorial, orchestrated by the blues Nazis who run Austin. But prison wisdom dictates that you don't fuck with an old wolf. Hear Ye Whomever Keith Has Offended: The man offers no apologies or regrets.

He welcomes me to his front porch, the center of his universe. His current band is the Solid Senders. Fronted by the singing dishwasher, they rarely work, particularly since Ferguson will only play cities south of Austin -- or Amsterdam. With its sane drug laws and hardly any cops, crime, poverty, or AIDS, Amsterdam is a tailor-made utopia. The Solid Senders did a blissful tour there. Ferguson pines to return: "If I hustled up some job washing dishes in Amsterdam -- hell, I'll supply the Palmolive -- we'd be back in a shot."

Ferguson, 49, was the founding bass player of both the Fabulous Thunderbirds and the Tail Gators, and played with a dozen Texas virtuosos in their formative years including Johnny Winter, Stevie Ray Vaughan, and Junior Brown. "He's a cracker's cracker," Ferguson says of his old boss Brown. "Thinks that Waylon and them are commie fags." Ferguson keeps a band honest. When he departed the T-Birds, that band was ready to compromise and play the pop charts; he'd have none of it.

No bass player ever layered so much bottom. Ferguson's trademark wasn't licks, riffs, slapping, or thumb popping -- just a swinging elephant trunk of bottom beneath every song. This deceptive gift earned him a lower pedigree than "musician's musician," itself a poverty-stricken but honorable curse: Ferguson is a bass player's bassist.

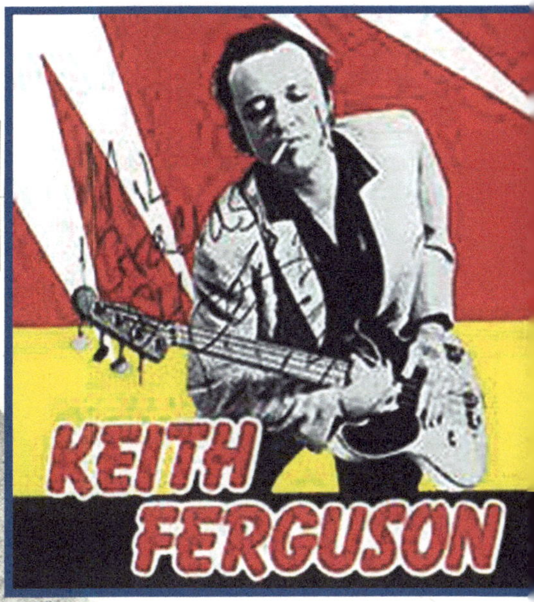
KEITH
FERGUSON

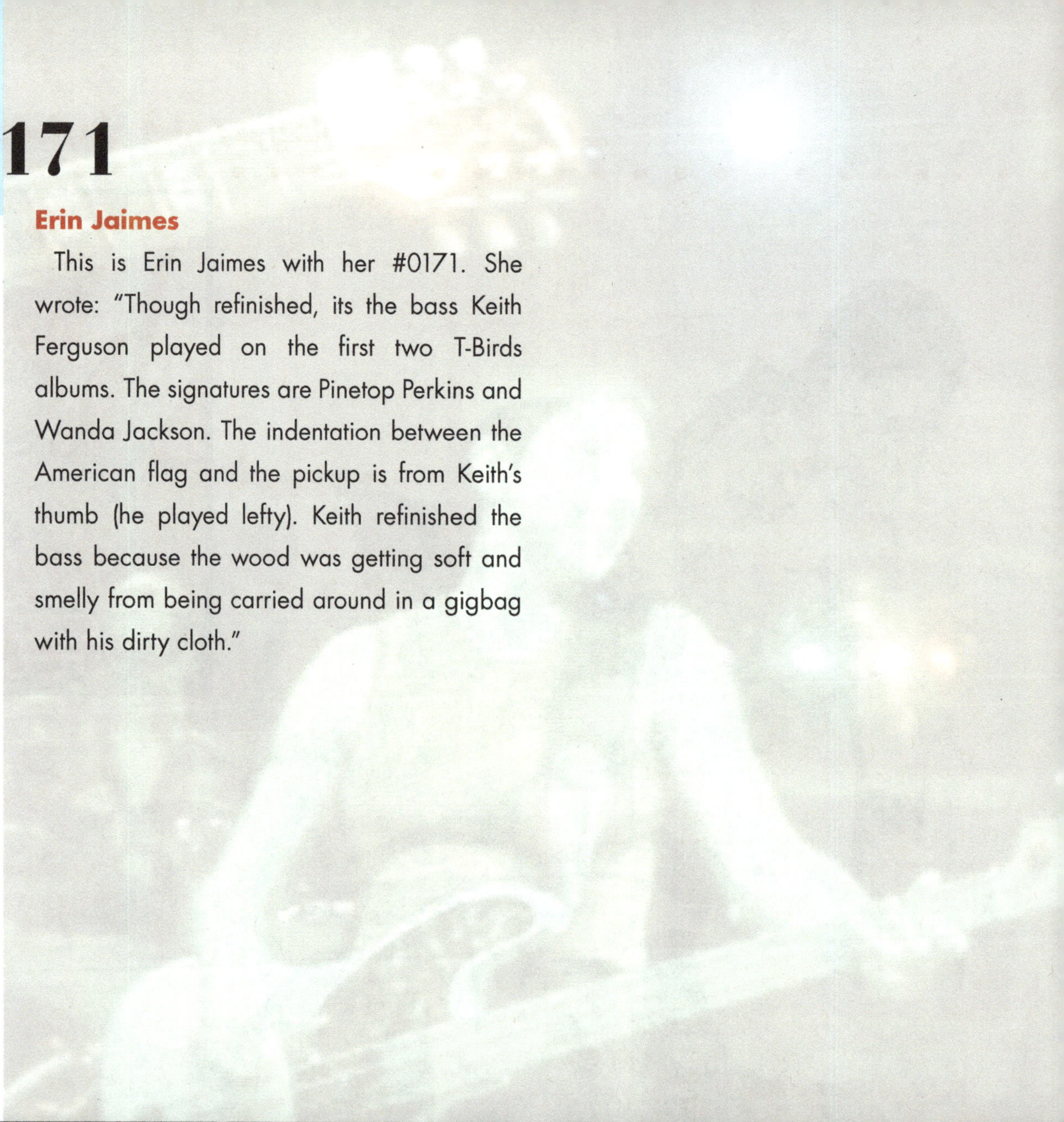

#0171

Erin Jaimes

This is Erin Jaimes with her #0171. She wrote: "Though refinished, its the bass Keith Ferguson played on the first two T-Birds albums. The signatures are Pinetop Perkins and Wanda Jackson. The indentation between the American flag and the pickup is from Keith's thumb (he played lefty). Keith refinished the bass because the wood was getting soft and smelly from being carried around in a gigbag with his dirty cloth."

#0256

Preston Hubbard

This is Preston Hubbard and his #0256. He sent me some close ups and wrote:"When I got her, she was pristine...brand new. I put the wear and tear on her over the years. I still have the original tweed case and booklet stored. The case is in excellent shape b/c I never use it. The tweed case even had the price tag on it. I have never taken the neck off or hardware or anything. Just the pickup cover. It got in the way. She has never been touched except for playing. Clifford Antone gave it to me in the late 80s. His legacy to me."

Many photos show him playing this bass (T-Birds, Lou Ann Barton, Tony Vega Band, Shawn Pittmann etc.,etc). See his website - www.prestonhubbard.com .

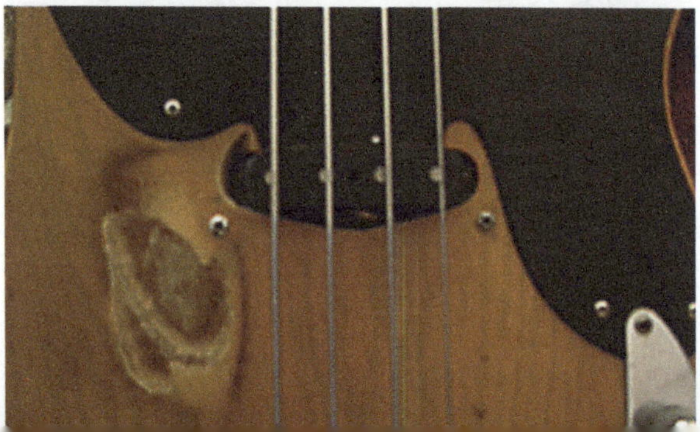

#0011

Here we start with "Basses by Serial Numbers". # 0011 is the lowest I have seen on a picture.

This bass once belonged to Guy Pratt, the bass player of Pink Floyd, Icehouse, Roxy Music and others. It is even mentioned in his book "My bass and other animals".

Fender
PRECISION BASS

EM
11-17-51

0011

#0036

This bass belongs to my friend Dave. One out of 83 that were sold in 1951. Dave was told by Richard Smith that only 19 basses were shipped to Texas in 1951 to a shop named McCord. The bodydate of #0036 is Nov-6-51. If you look close in the neck pocket it says Guitar Test and Austin, Texas. And it has the name "Gonzales" written in the neck pocket too.

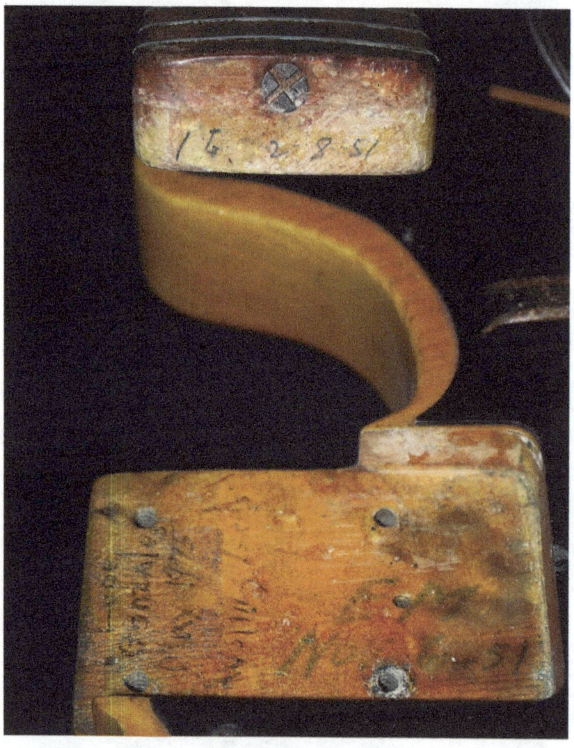

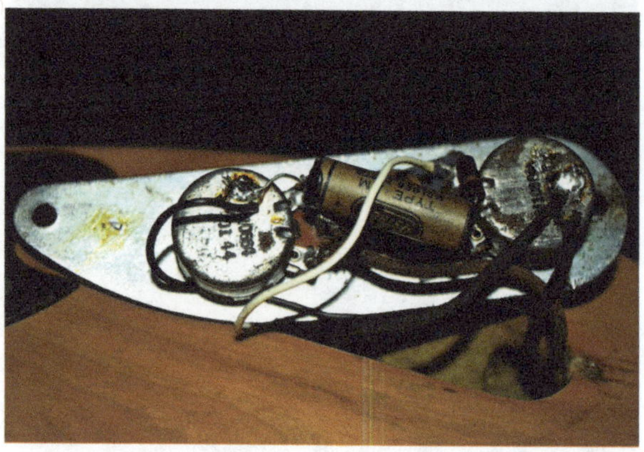

0036

FENDER

#0038

These pictures were sent to me by Pat from "This Old Guitar". This '52 bass is all original except a little routing in the control cavity, and possibly a changed pot. This may be factory work, as Pat says there is colour over the routing.

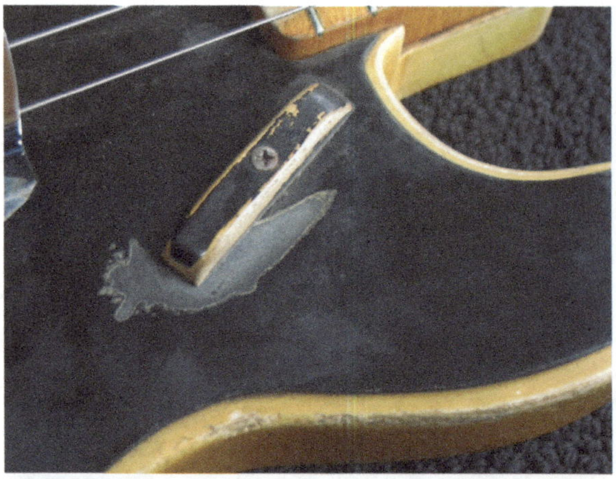

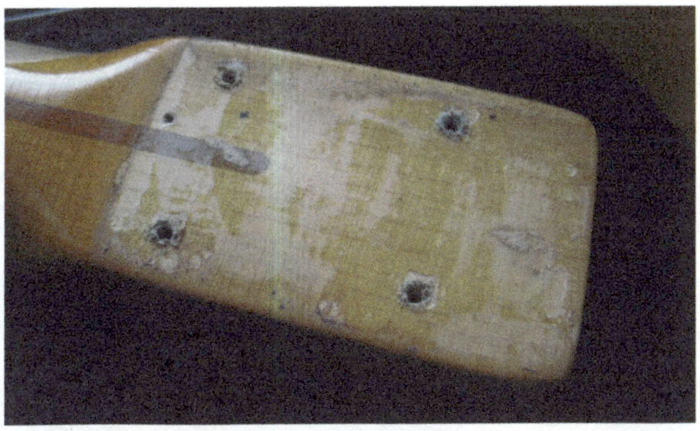

TG 4-29-52

#0038

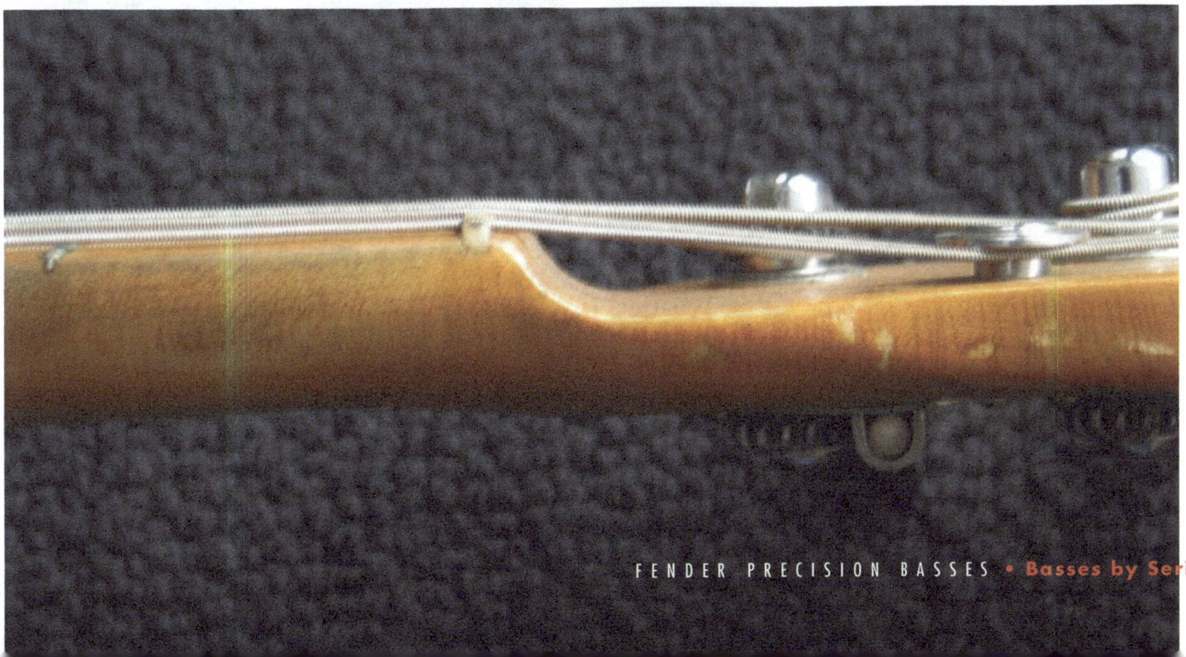

#0042

#0042 has the neck date 11-19-51. It came from JK Lutherie who found it in the garage of a guitar repairman who had died and whose widow then sold it. It was complete except for the pickguard and the pickup was dead. The neck was extensively damaged and Dave had to have it professionally reworked.

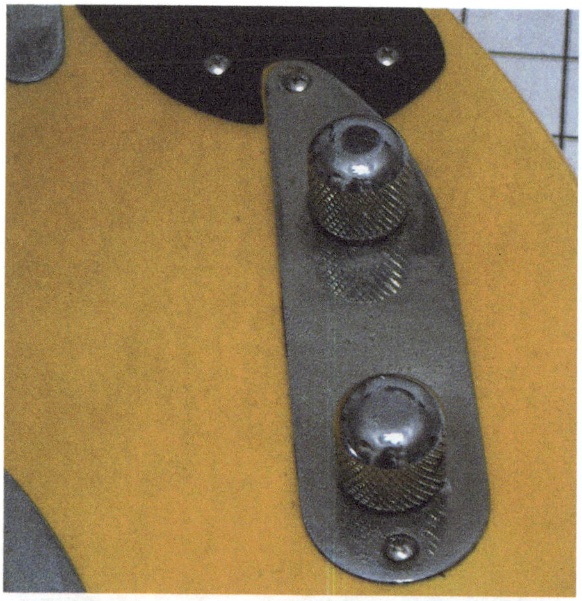

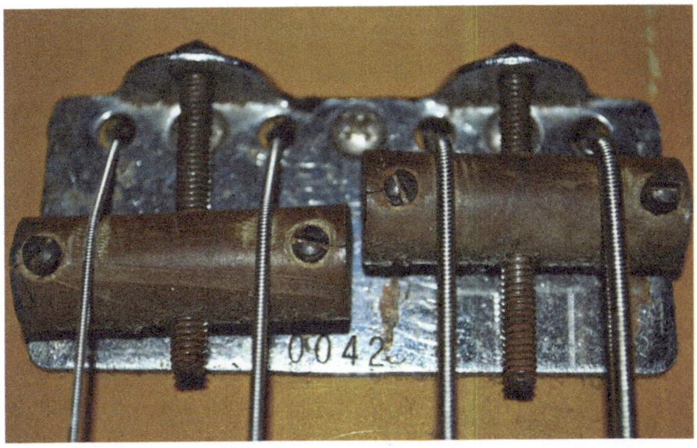

#0052

This is a perfect example of a '52 P-Bass. It even included the bag. I just love the look of this bass. Neck date: 7-21-52, Body date 9-2-52. These pictures were given to me by Roland, the publisher of the German bass magazine "Bass Professor".

The new owner had restored it, mainly the fretboard.

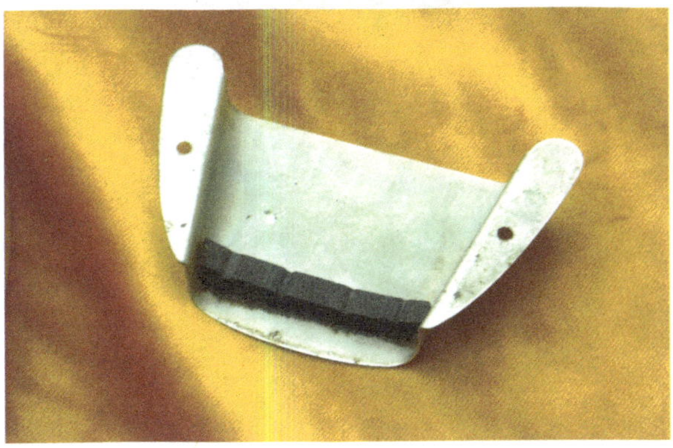

#0064

#0064 belonged to my friend George and was born 1-28-52. By coincidence, George was the first person I met, who also had a 1952 Fender Bass. Since then, we have had many interesting discussions. So this bass is a twin brother to my #0272, born on the same day. This again exemplifies the random assignation of serial numbers, as it is a safe assumption that 208 basses were not made on the same day, between these two.

Johnny Horton and his Band. Note: a Fender bass and upright bass on the same stage!

#0144

This is maybe the most discussed bass on the Fender Forum. The owner made the most detailed photos that I ever saw. It has a '51 neck and a body that was painted in 1954. Its a "one owner bass" and documented since it was bought in 1955.

Original words of the seller: "My Mother purchased this bass from the Walter D. Moses Company in Richmond, VA after learning how to play on the stand-up "bass fiddle" (as it was referred to then). Having grown tired of lugging around and playing an upright bass, she was impressed by the idea of an electric bass and purchased this one in June of 1955 with an initial payment of $50, the balance of $149.50 being paid in August of 1955. She and my Dad were founding members of a group called The Country Cavaliers. They were the house band at the New Dominion Barn Dance, held

originally in the LyricTheatre in downtown Richmond, VA from 1957 - 1967. This band (and therefore this bass) shared the stage with many Nashville stars."

"The serial number [0144] is located on the bridge plate and, curiously, stamped on the

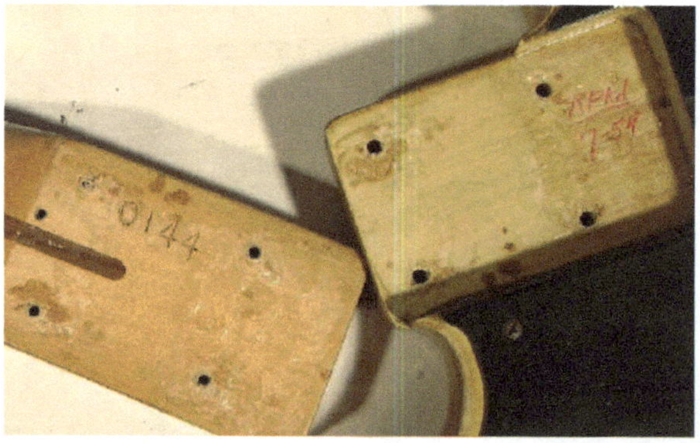

bottom of the neck itself. Even more curious is the penciled date of 9-18-51 on the butt of the neck and 7-54 on the neck slot of the body. In the control cavity, the masking tape has "Virginia 9-13-54" clearly written on it. Then, it would seem that this instrument was built in 1954 with a neck from 1951."

"Evidence is still emerging that this instrument must be older than a 1954 model and was possibly one of the original 83 1951's that was sent back to the factory for some sort of repair or refinishing before being shipped to Walter D. Moses in Richmond, VA in 1955 as a "new" bass.

1-The impression of a milled jack cup (only found in 1951 basses) in the outer jack cavity, also the copper jack retainer I'm told was only on the earliest basses.

2-Neck initialled by Tadeo Gomez 9-18-51 dates neck to about a month before Fender installed the machinery to make them - possibly making this one a hand made prototype

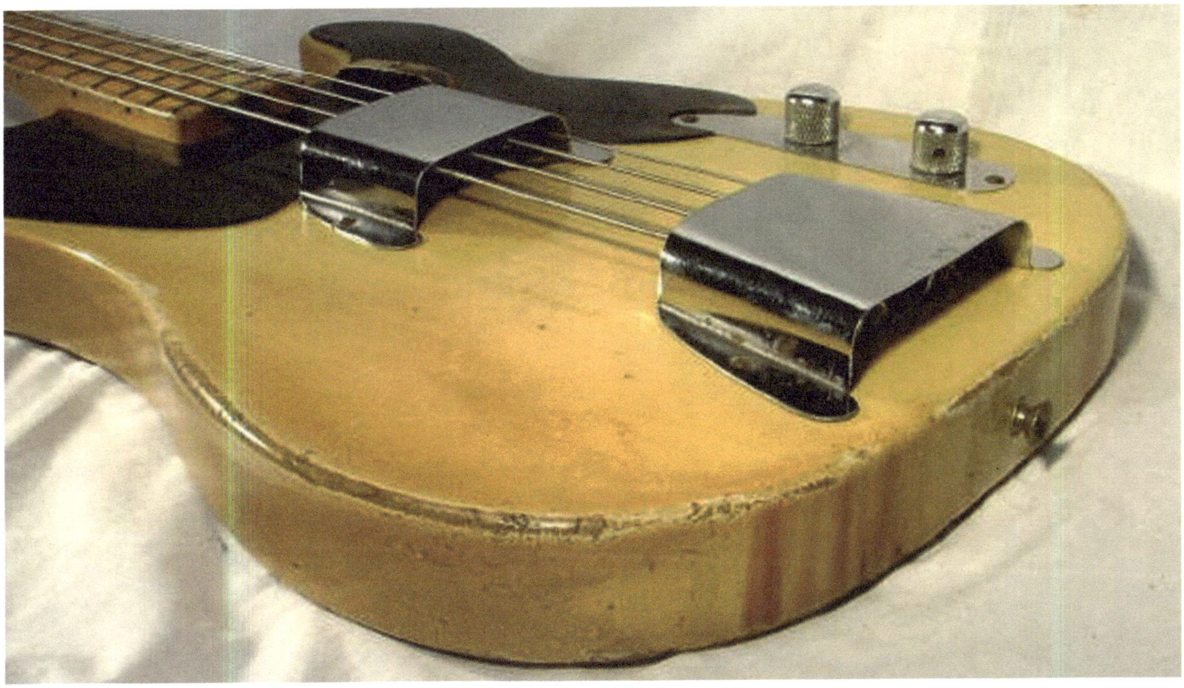

3-Low [0144] serial number

4-Extra set of 7 unused holes under the pickguard."

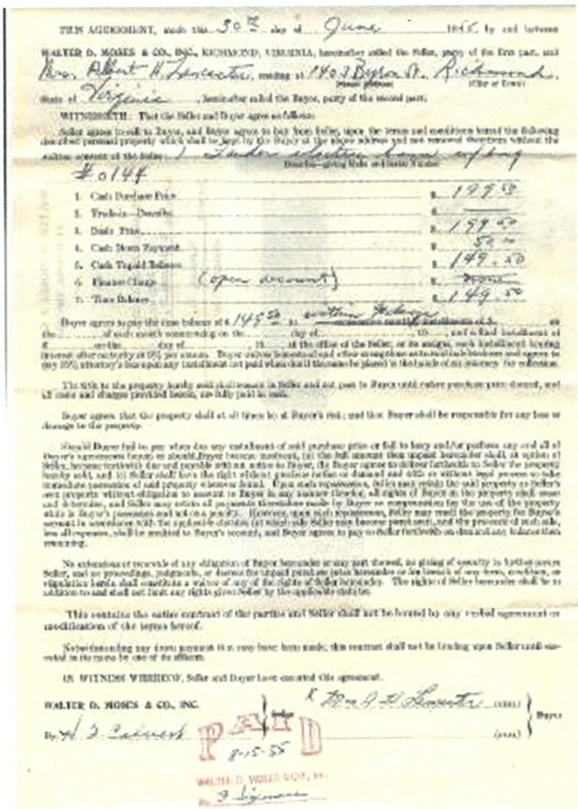

THIS AGREEMENT, made this 30th day of June 1955, by and between WALTER D. MOSES & CO., INC., RICHMOND, VIRGINIA, hereinafter called the Seller, party of the first part, and Mrs. Albert H. Lancaster, residing at 1403 Byron St. Richmond, State of Virginia, hereinafter called the Buyer, party of the second part.

WITNESSETH: That the Seller and Buyer agree as follows:

[illegible]

1 Fender electric bass & case #0144

1.	Cash Purchase Price	$ 199.50
2.	Trade-in—Describe	$ —
3.	Sale Price	$ 199.50
4.	Cash Down Payment	$ 50.00
5.	Cash Unpaid Balance	$ 149.50
6.	Finance Charge (open account)	$ [illegible]
7.	Time Balance	$ 149.50

[illegible]

IN WITNESS WHEREOF, Seller and Buyer have executed this agreement.

WALTER D. MOSES & CO., INC.

By [illegible]

PAID 8-15-55

#0144

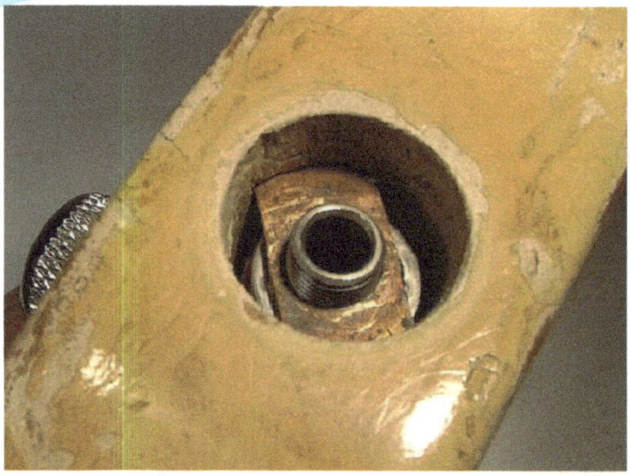

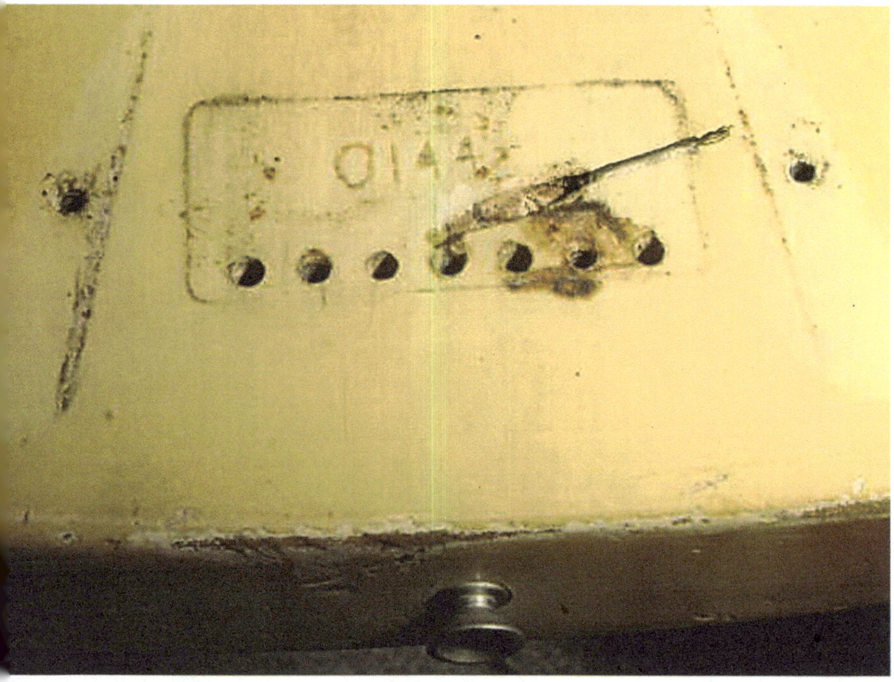

Another interesting feature that I discovered later on his #0144 bass, is that the bigger routing for the ground wire is missing. For me, this is a sign that this bass indeed is a very early model and body and neck go together well, looking at all the different pictures.

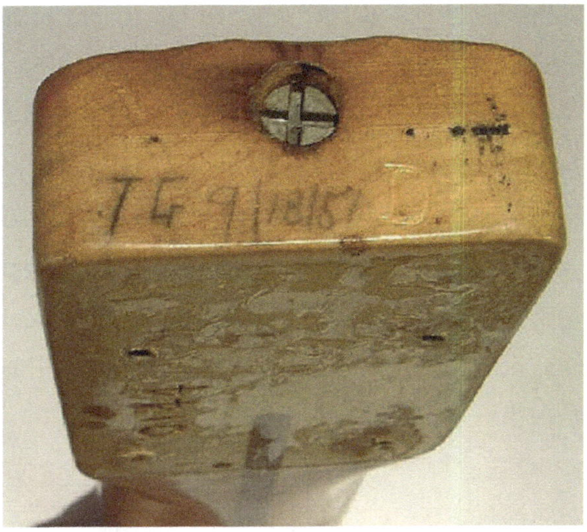
TG 9/18/57 D

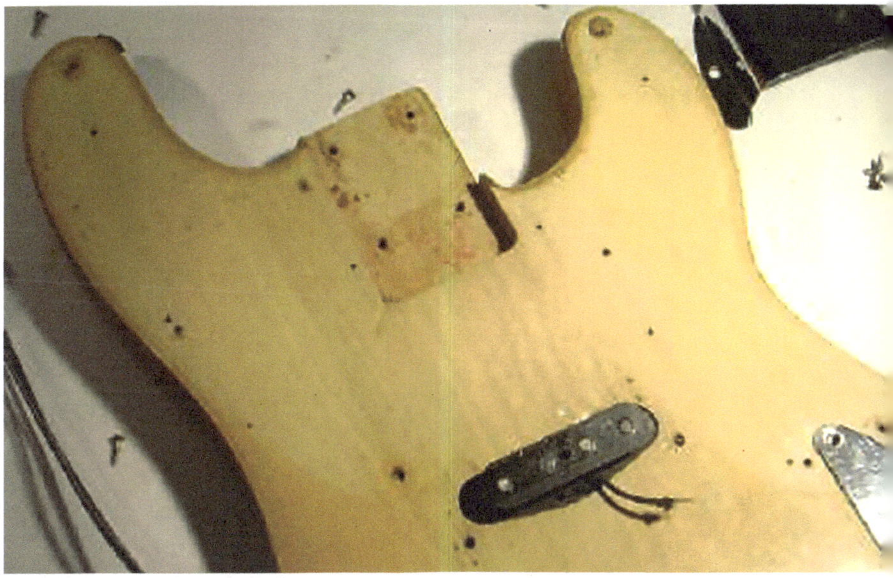

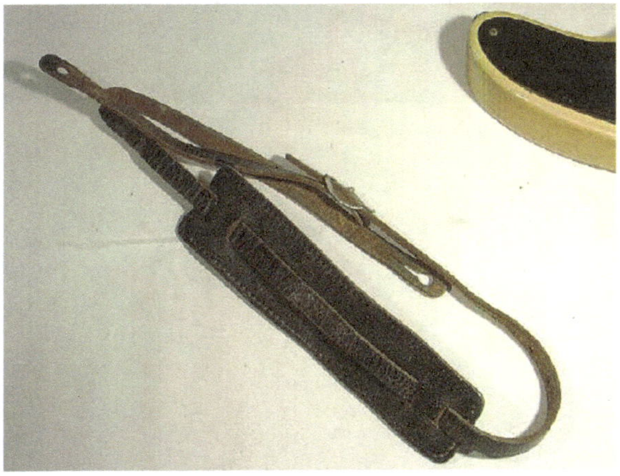

#0153

This bass has a sad story to tell: once in its lifetime it had block markers installed. They were later changed back to dots, the work is hard to detect from any distance. It belonged to Kim Wilson's bass player. Note the neck also was made 4-1-52; Tadeo Gomez ("TG") used red ink. The backside of the bass is in almost original condition, but the front is stripped. This bass has a milled jack cup.

#0215

This bass belongs to J.B. Note the bodydate 7-7-52 with the name "Eddie", most likely for Eddie Miller. Also for the first time I have seen the E.M.#8 signature.

Neckdate is 7-15-52. Pickup wiring is new, altough most likely the pickup has been changed.

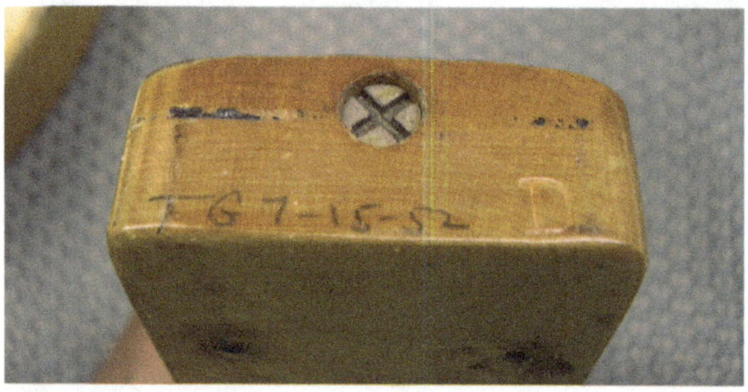

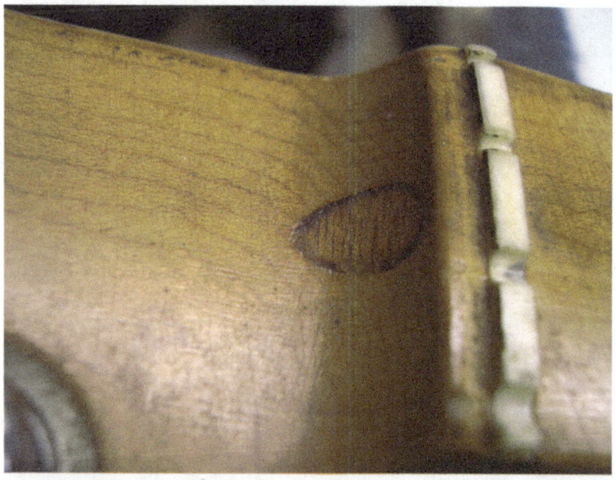

FENDER
0215

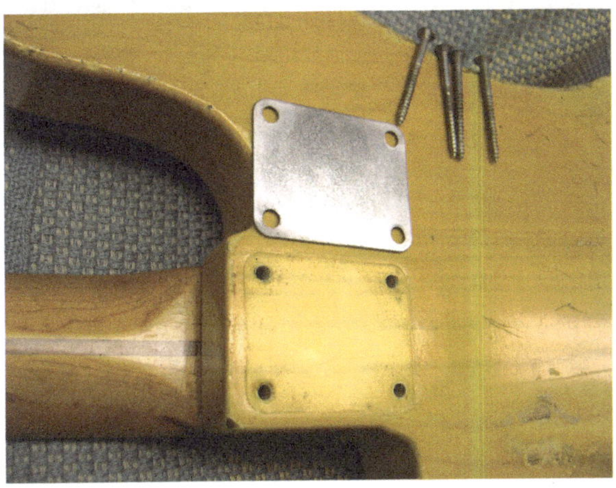

#0220

This beauty belongs to Ken, who has quite a good collection. This bass is also pictured in Nacho Banos' book "The Blackguard". Note the D-stamp on the neck. The mysterious stamp often appeared on neck and body on the early slab basses.

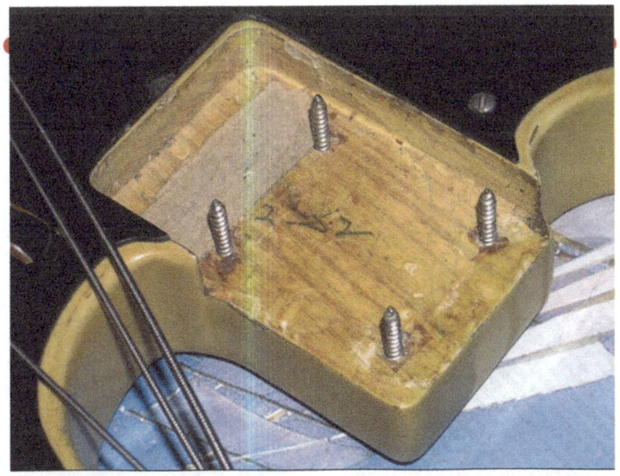

#0221

This '52 bass sounds very good even though it has a replacement Seymour Duncan pickup. Seymour Duncan makes some great pickups. I especially like his Antiquity line.

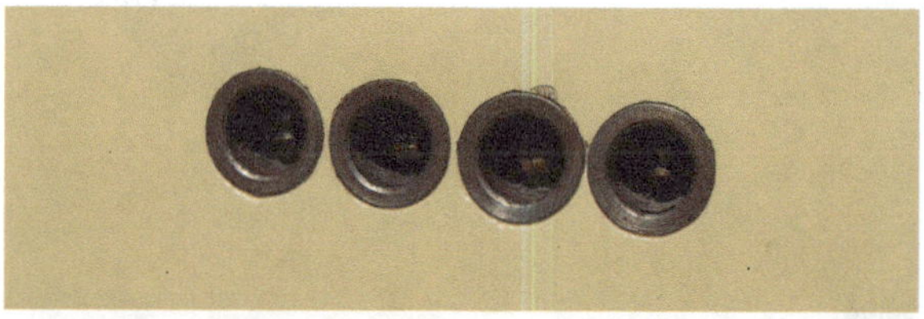

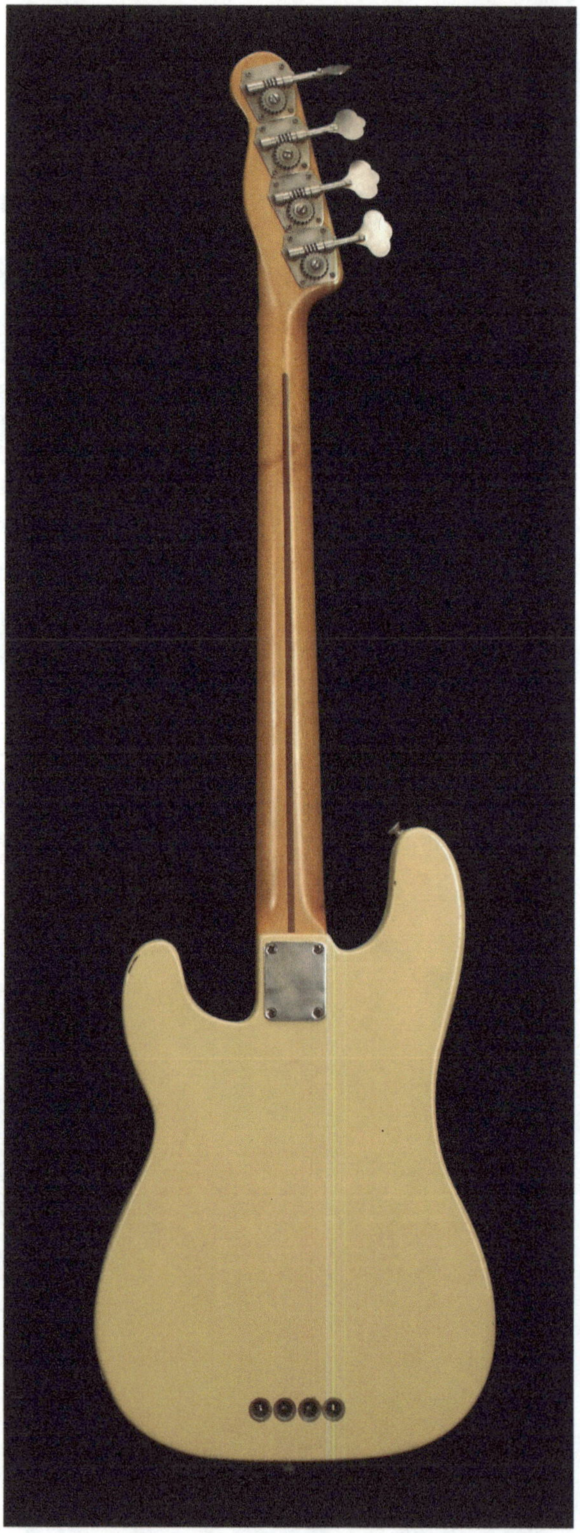

#0239

Thanks to Joe from Axe-Zactly Music for letting me use the photos of his 52 P-Bass:

"I purchased this bass from the original owner here in New Jersey, who purchased it from a very small music store in Camden NJ in 1952. This bass I am told is one of the very first Fender instruments ever sold on the East Coast of the USA through a retail music store. I was told that Leo Fender was selling mostly direct back then, and mostly West Coast sales. The original owner purchased this exact bass, and his bandmate purchased a Fender Telecaster from the same music store the same day."

"All the parts are original with exception of the pickguard screws. The original single-coil pickup was re-wound many years ago by Lindy Fralin, and has a strong, powerful output. It was missing its wooden thumb-rest when I got it. (There are two small holes that were added to the body top below the pickup. The original owner moved the position of the metal pickup cover to a slightly lower position. These can not be seen with the metal cover on). "

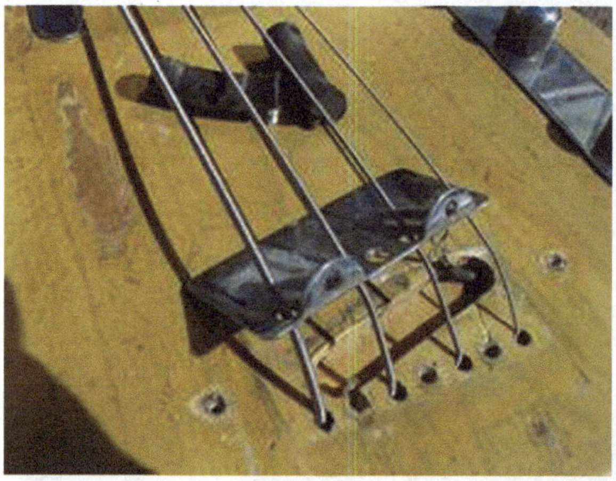

Most interesting is the dating of the neck cavity. Seems like the first date was erased, then a new date was added. A second D-stamp can be seen, most likely a proof that the D-stamp is a kind of a control-stamp that was added to body and neck in addition to the signature and date in the early 50s.

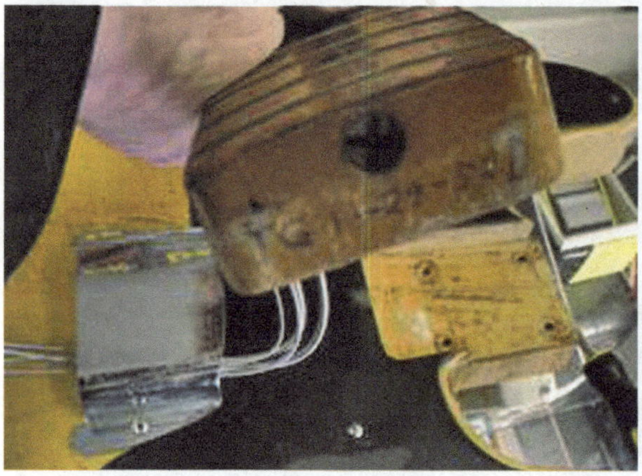

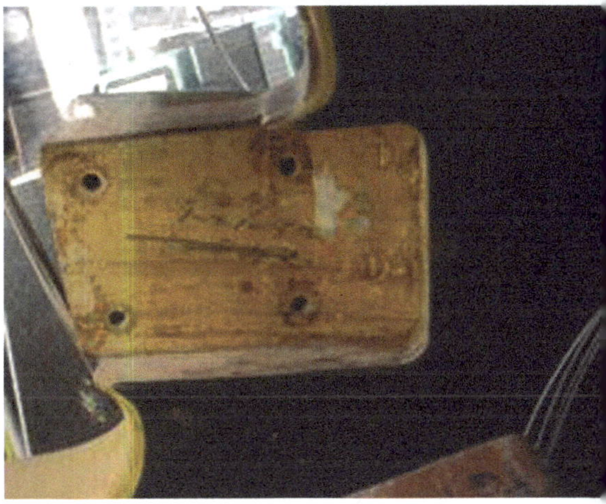

#0241

This Precision Bass was owned and played by Larry Taylor of Canned Heat.

The neck is dated in pencil: "TG 11-21-51" (Tadeo Gomez November 21, 1951) and has a "D" stamped in blind. The bottom of the neck is stamped in blind: "R & R 3228." The neck pocket is dated in pencil: "-- -- 51" and has "R & R 3228" stamped in blue.

Investigation: The #0241 Trail

My friend Dave did an intensive research on his #0241 bass, here is the story:

"I just got off the phone with Lloyd McKinney, Mabron's brother. The early bass player for Duwane and Greg Allman when they called themselves the Hour Glass. Larry told me he bought the 51 bass he had from Mabron in L.A. in 68 when they were both recording there. I finally tracked him down and his brother confirmed it. He also invited me over to Alabama to talk to Mabron, so I'm going there Saturday with his bass. I can't wait to hear the early Allman brothers stories, and all the others he played with like Percy Sledge, and others at Muscle Shoals studio. I also would like to know of the history of this 1951 pbass, which was modified by Fender in the fifties and painted blue"

"I just got back from Alabama. I spent the whole afternoon with Mabron listening to him talk about the early years as the Cavemen, The Five Minutes and with the Allmans and at the Muscle shoals studio"

"I had a wonderful time listening to Mabron, he has a tough time physically but he can remember some obscure details, like the knotholes and imperfections in the neck of his bass. So I know my bass was sent back to Fender and reshaped and painted blue at sometime and ended up at McCabe's Music shop in Longbeach in 1967. Its a shame McCabe died two weeks ago, this might be where the trail ends."

"Mabron told me, he and the Allmans moved out to L.A. and moved in with the Nitty Gritty Dirt band to record an album with Liberty records. He said that his bass and Duwane's guitar were stolen just after they got there. Jimmy Fadden said he knew where a cool old bass was and he drove to McCabe's Music shop in Longbeach and there on the wall was a blue 1951 custom modified Fender Bass, so Mabron bought it for 375 dollars. All of his recordings and concerts were done with that bass, he played all over L.A. with a lot of local musicians."

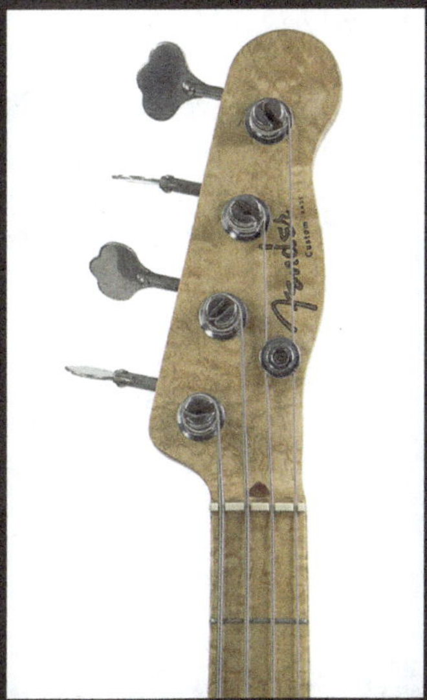

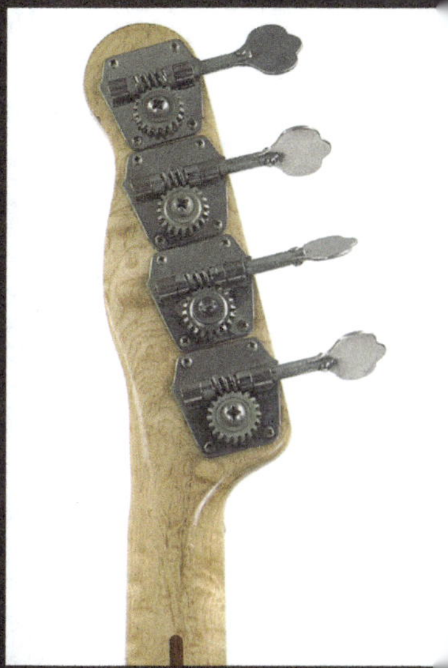

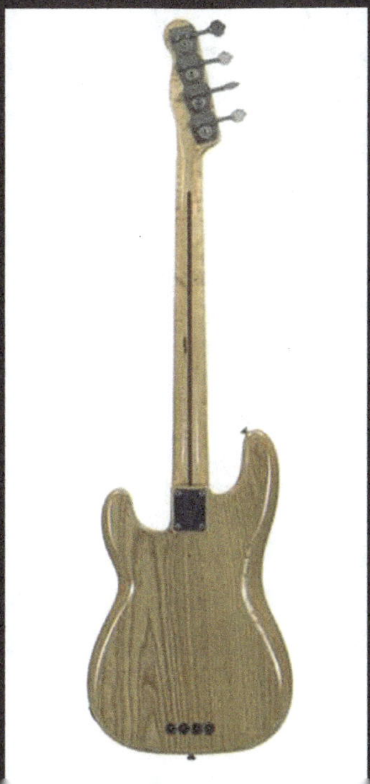

#0241

"When he saw my/his bass, it brought him to tears. He left L.A. and brought the bass back to Alabama and continued playing in studios in Muscle Shoals with a lot of southern rock musicians. He said he sold it to Larry Taylor with whom he became friends with in L.A. in New Orleans at some concert."

"Mabron's mother was a sweet southern lady and took me to the old club Mabron played at while in the Cavemen and The 5 Minutes and with the Allmans in the Hourglass, it has long since been closed and was out in the most rural Alabama country. Just a little bit of rock and roll history"

Added by the author: The Cavemen were a band, where Scotty Moore played guitar.

First club

Mabron and his 51

#0264

This is a refinished 1951 bass. It now belongs to Dave. He bought it in a parking lot in Miami. Note the writing in the neck pocket: Eddie Miller, I had always thought, Eddie was Eddie Mendoza, but wrong.

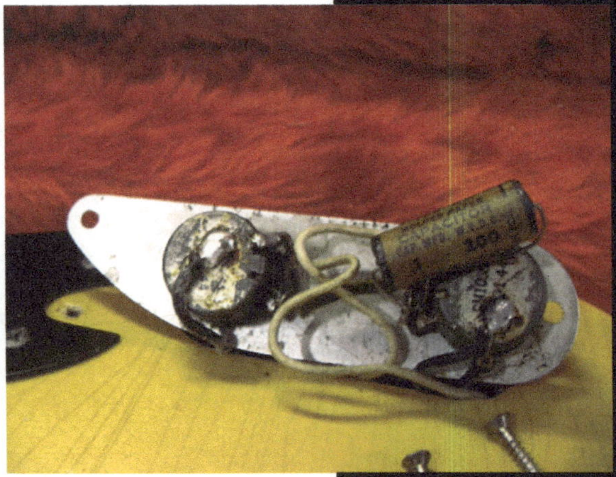

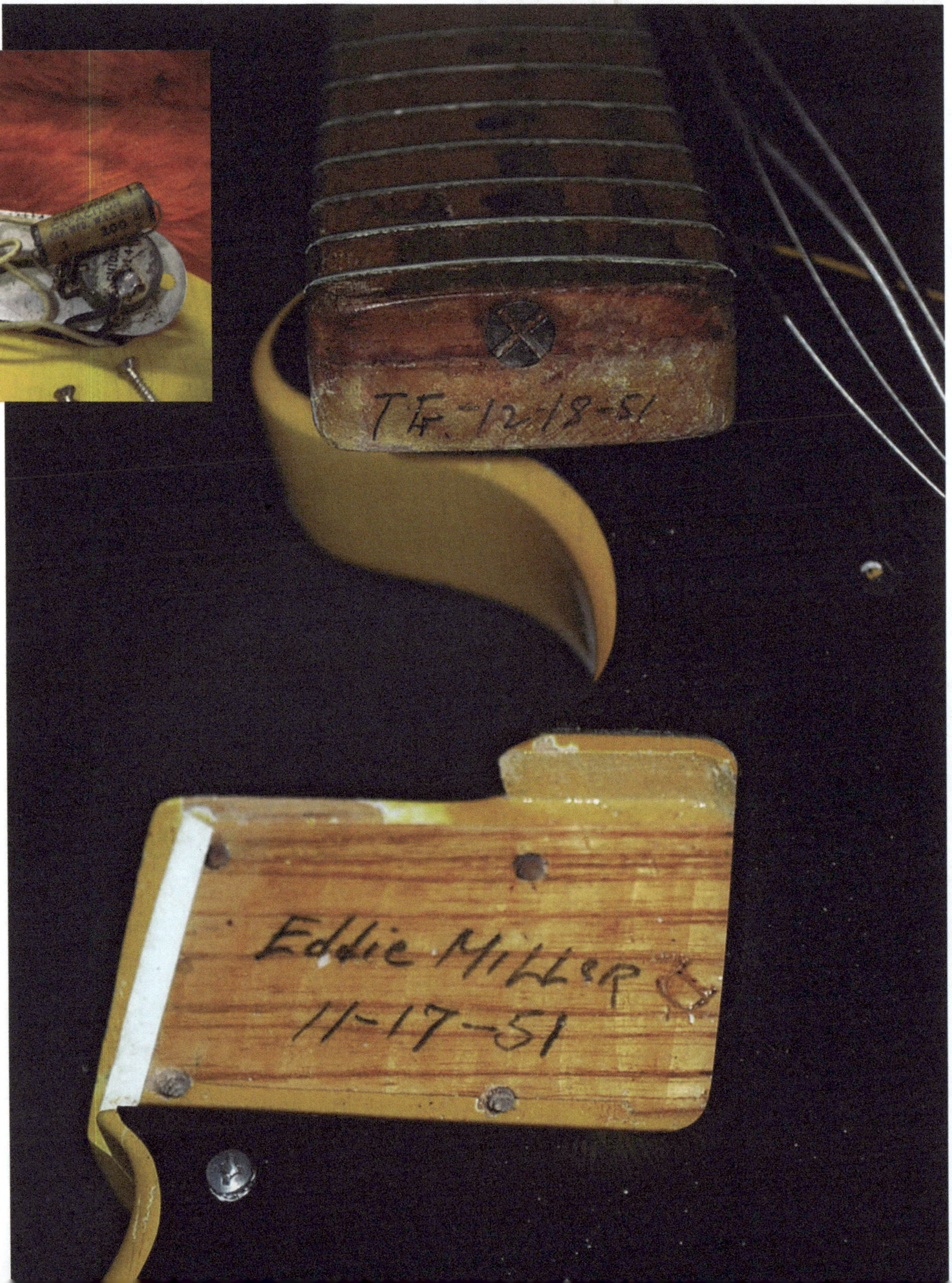

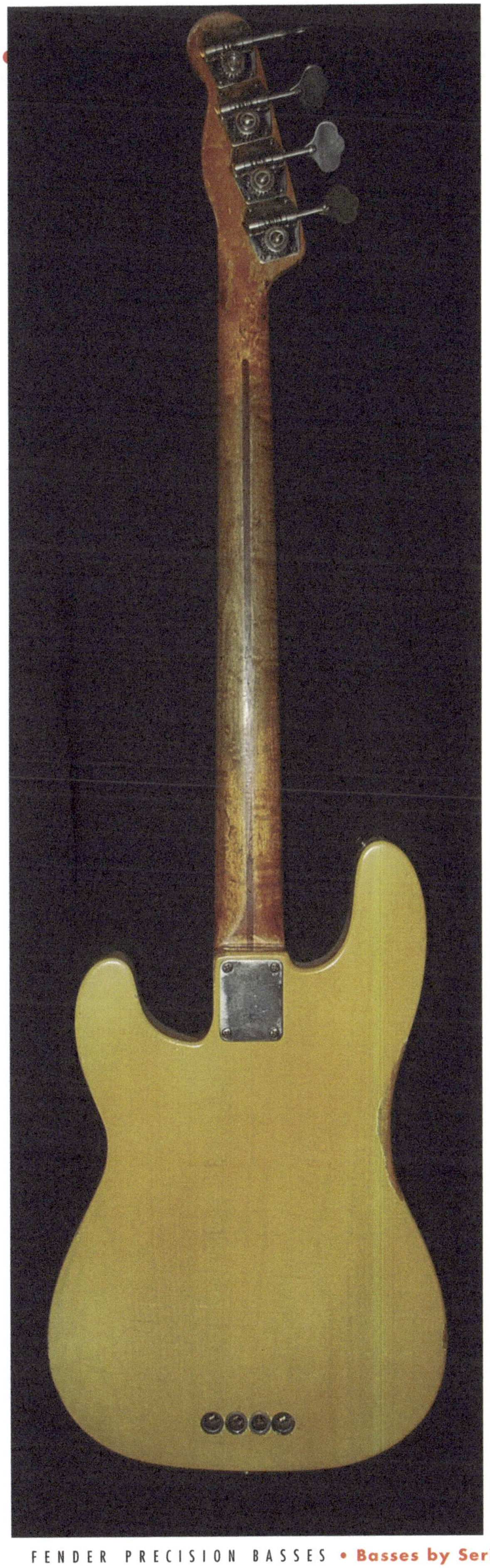

#0272

This is the twin brother of #0064, born on the same day 1-28-52. It was later carved, a Guild Humbucker installed (sounds great) and factory refinished in Candy Apple Red in the late 1960s. It belonged to an Army musician who bought it in 1952 in New York. This bass has seen the world.

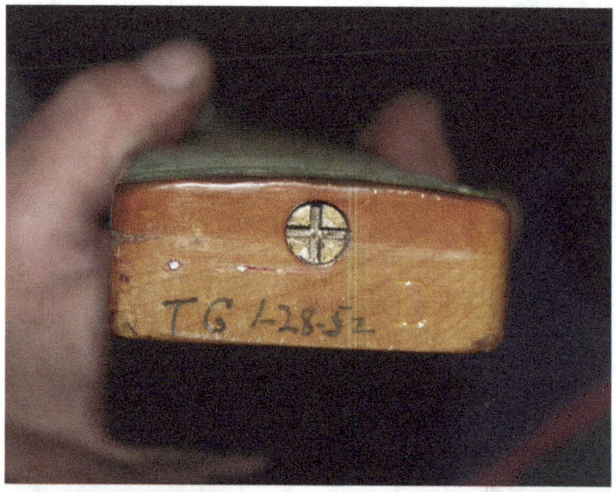

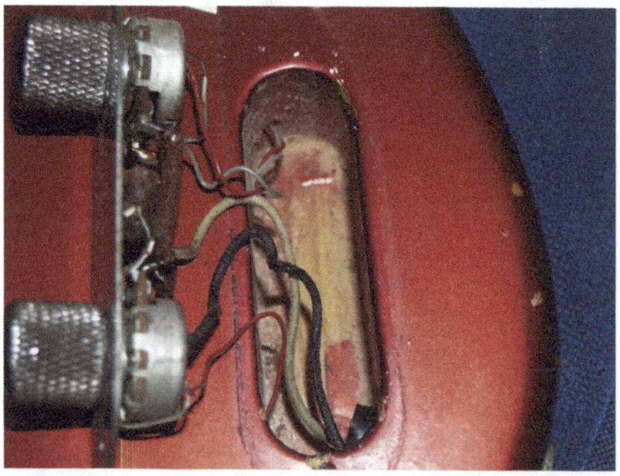

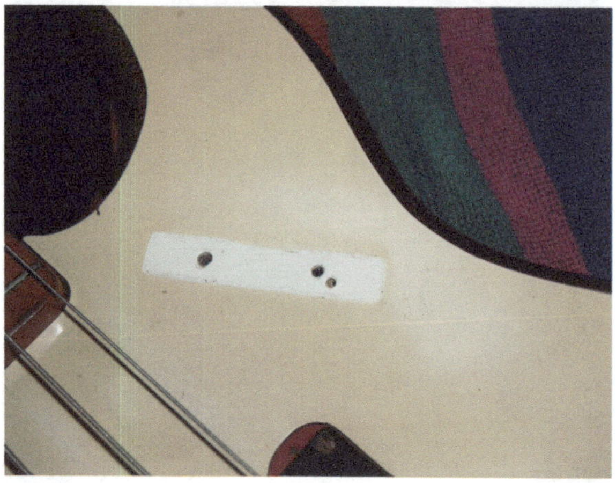

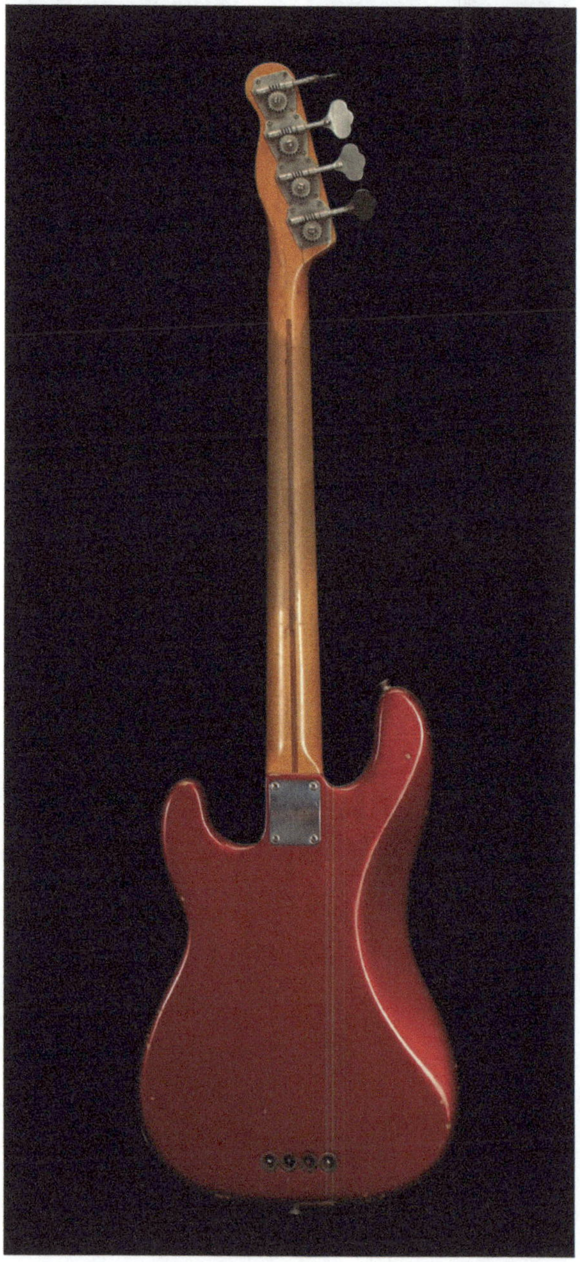

W 28-72

#0284

This 52 P-bass had belonged to my friend Erwin, who used to have a large collection of Fender Basses. It was in fantastic original condition when he possessed it. Sadly he had to sell all of his basses. But he gave me the photo he made in the 80s and let me use it in this book (tree photo). During my research I found the new owner Bernard Groll, musician and collector, who sent me new photos.

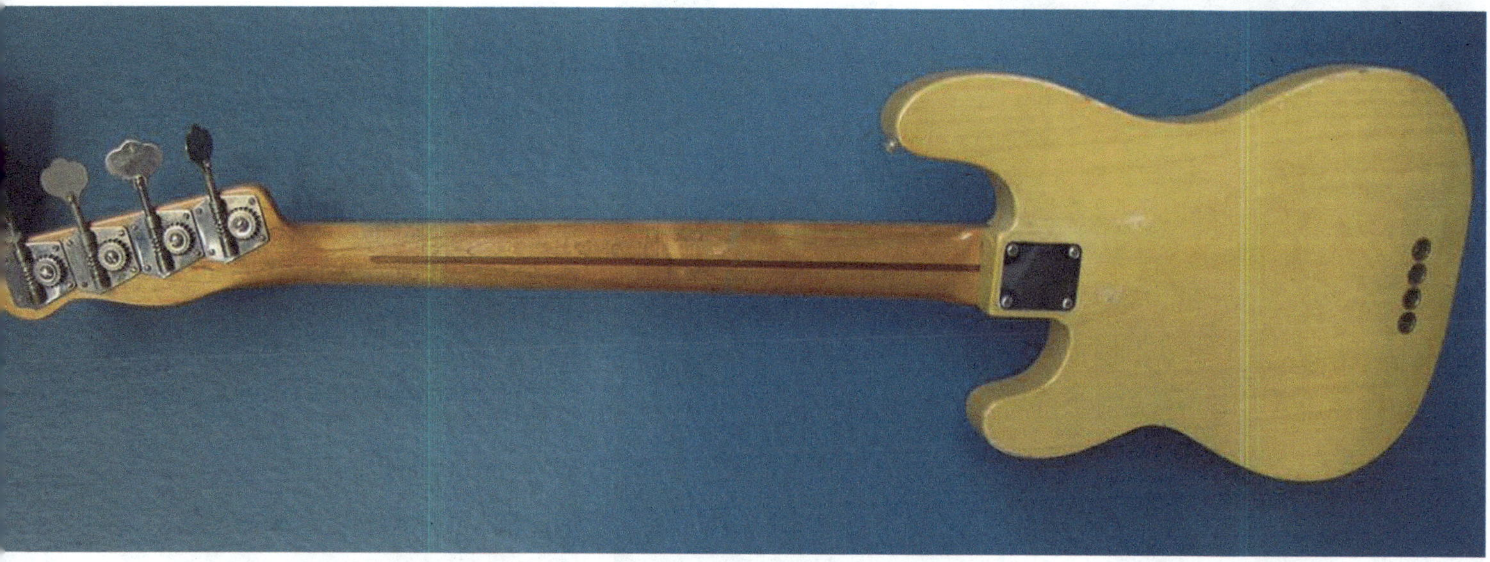

Fender
PRECISION BASS

#0287

This is a 1952 Precision bass.

It is totally original except the mounting screws of the pickup and the screws of the bridge. Note the coloration of the body.

Neck date is 4-24-52, body date is 3-17-52. It has the D-stamp in the neck pocket.

TG 4-24-52

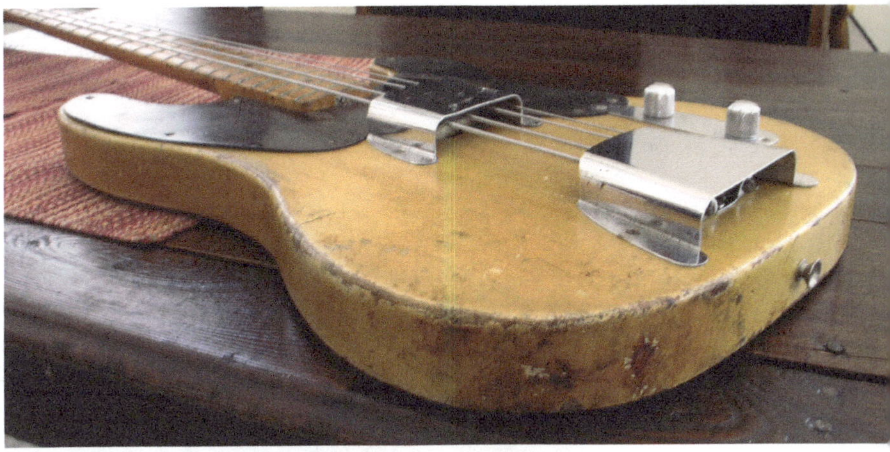

#0368

This bass belongs to Heinz in Germany. It is listed in the Werner list as built in December 1951.

#0386

This bass belongs to Albert Molinaro, the author of the book "The Fender Bass". Albert is a very friendly and helpful person. His book is very much recommended.

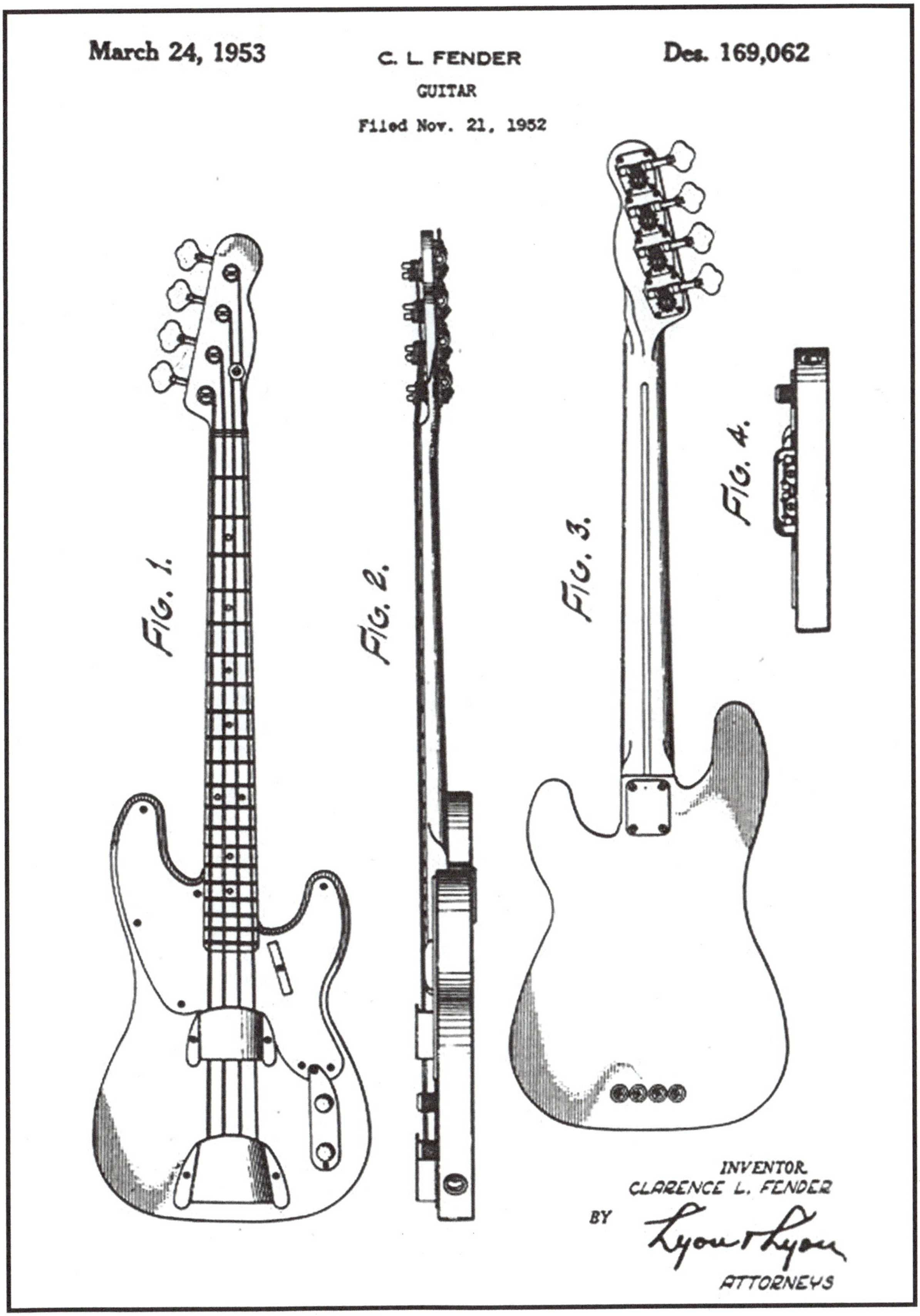

Early Fender design patent drawing

#0388

For some reason this is one of my best sounding, best playing basses. It's not the original pickup and the phenolic saddles are partly broken. I love it. Born on April 1st '52. Note the red ink Tadeo has used on this and a few others. XXX - with love from Tadeo. It has one of the biggest necks I have ever played.

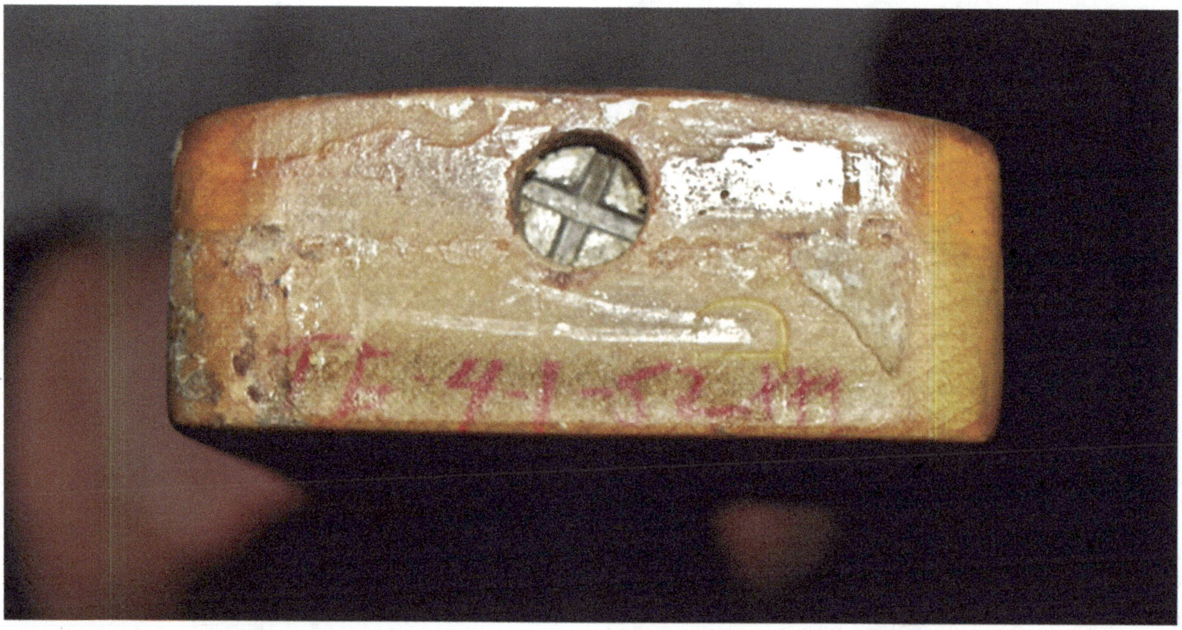

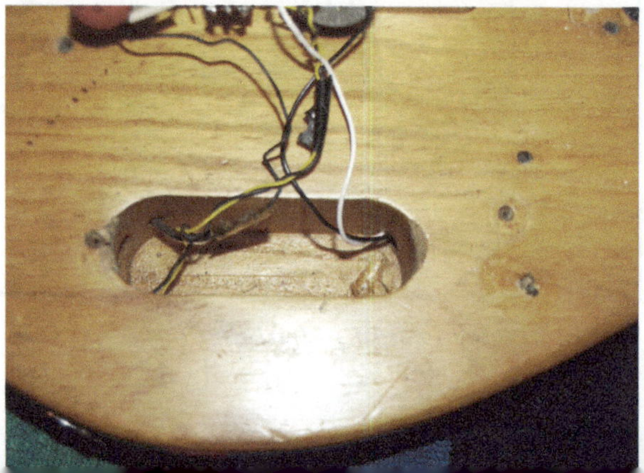

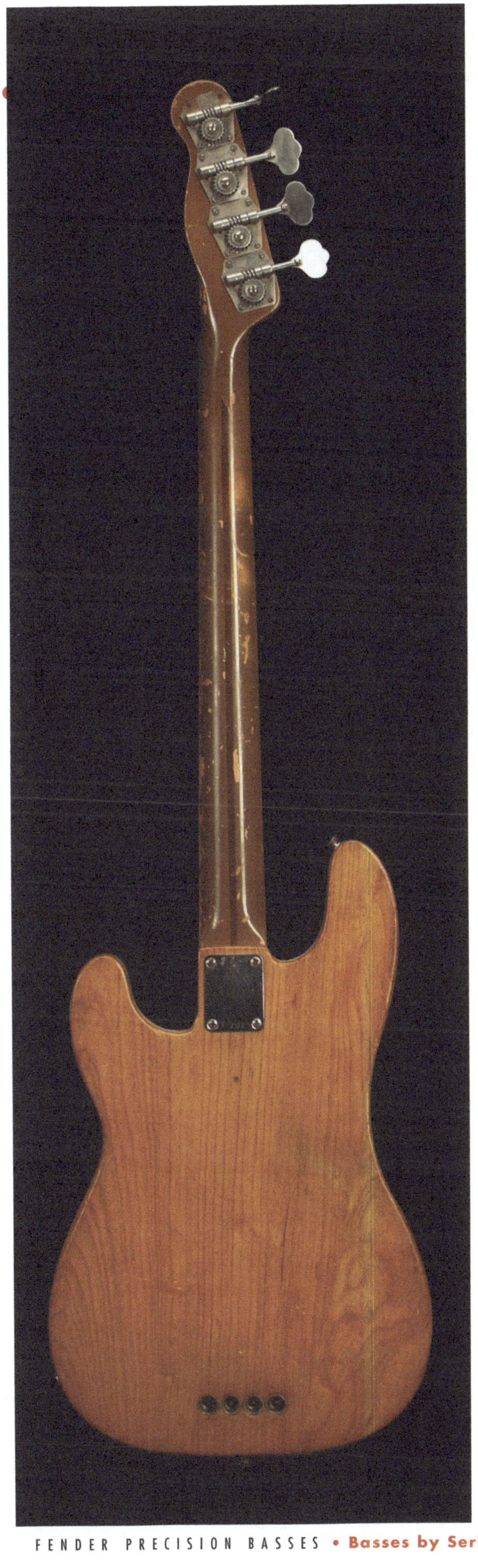

#0396

This bass was played a lot by a country musician named Billy Lewis. He played with many big country artists, including Lefty Frizell and Merle Haggard. With the bass came a letter from his wife detailing Billy's life and career.

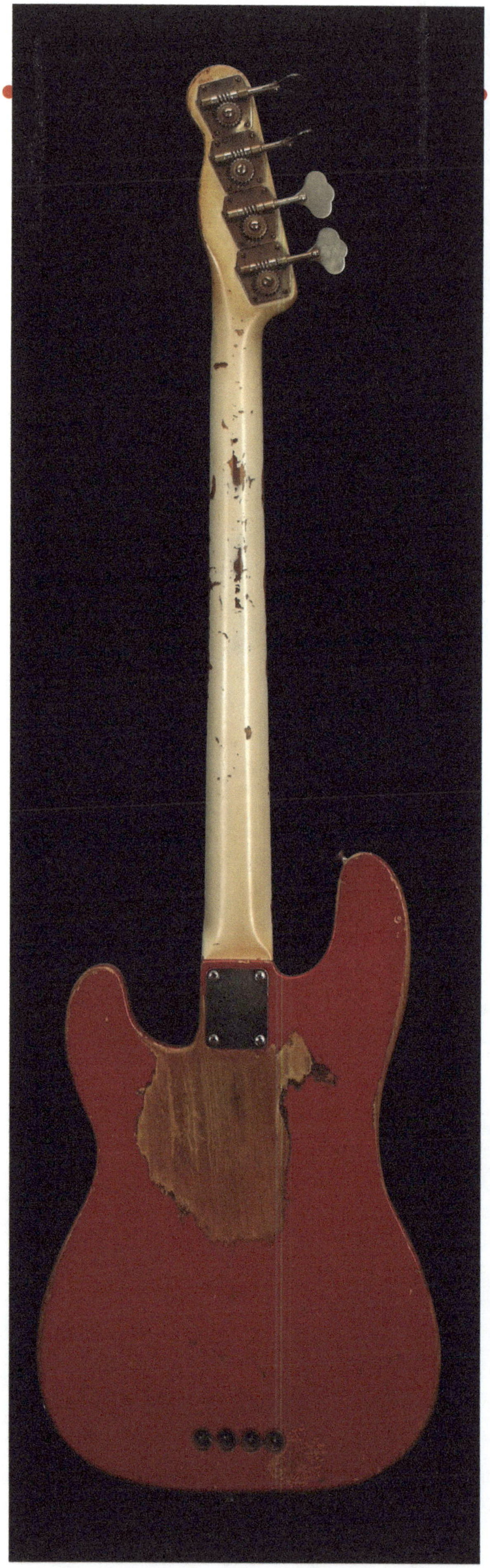

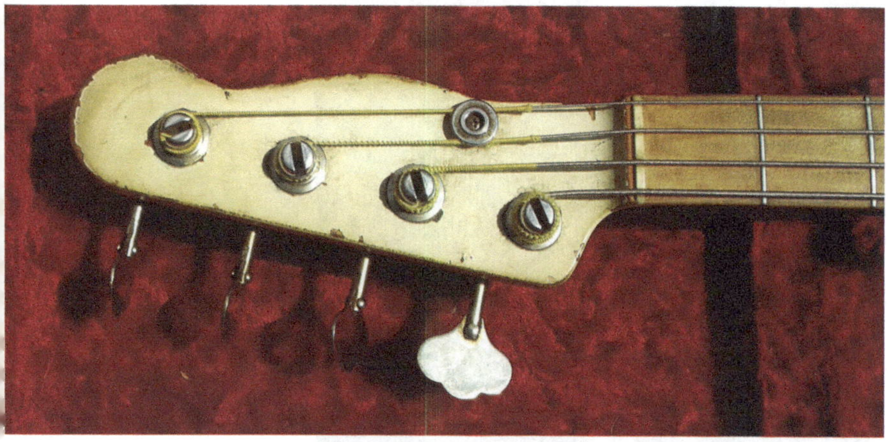

#0427

This bass belongs to Ben, who sent me lots of photos. This bass was a candidate for restoration. The bass has been through a fire at some point.

The pickup looks to have 7 magnets, but Ben wrote that it was only screws. Clearly visible is the D-stamp.

The neck was painted on the fretboard and also painted red on the backside, it has a new pickguard to fit the missing wood and lost some weight during a fire. Ben restored it back to a slab body. He sent me a photo of the restored bass. The paint job was done by J. Black. It is great work. Ben saved a vintage bass.

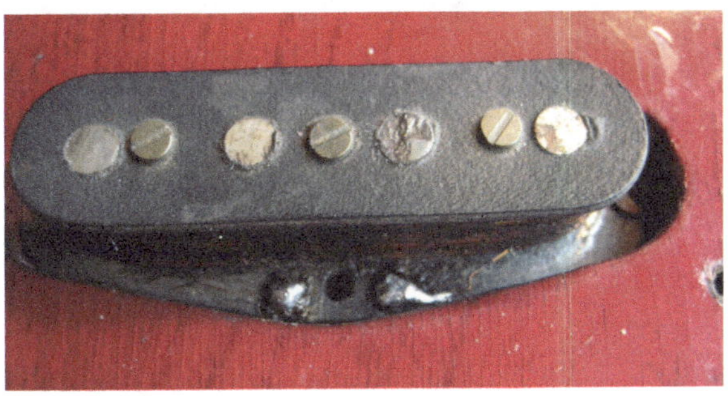

#0436

Once offered for sale on Ebay, this bass has a Nov-7-51 body date. It now belongs to my friend Dave.

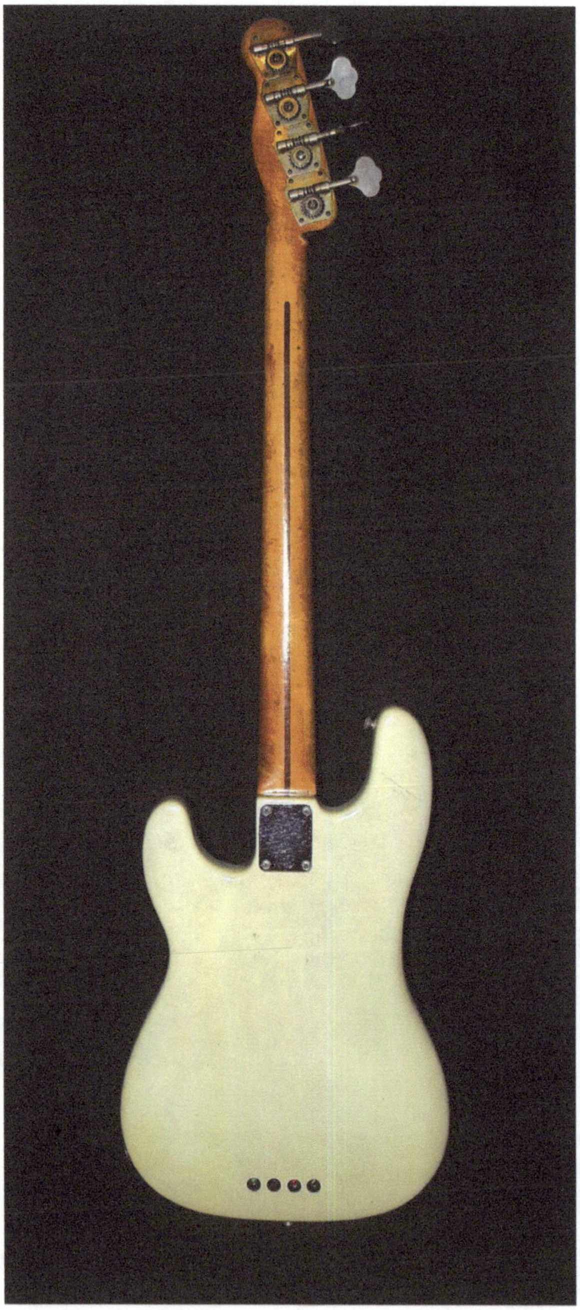

#0444

My friend Tony proudly presents his '52 P-Bass. It has the body date 9-5-52 and the neck date TG 9-26-52. This bass has seen many blues sessions. It is refinished on the body, and the neck seems to be oversprayed.

Mountaineer Playboys, 1958

L to R: Aaron Lee (electric guitar, electric mandolin, vocals) Loren Ross (guitar, vocals) "Kotten" (bass)

Venue: The Scenic Lounge, Milwaukee, Wisconsin USA. Located on 5th Street, north of Wisconsin Avenue, across from the Miller High Life Spa.

Aaron's guitar is a Fender electric with a Fender electric mandolin bolted to the guitar, making a "custom" double-neck instrument. Loren plays a Gretsch hollow body guitar. "Kotten's" bass is a 1955 or 1956 Fender Precision Bass

#0550

A 1955 bass that is still using the bridge where the serial number is stamped on. There must have been a lot of leftover bridges that Fender now used on the new contoured model. It still has the original tweed case with it. The case is really worn. The pickup cavity is a little bit routed. Note the first version of the logo.

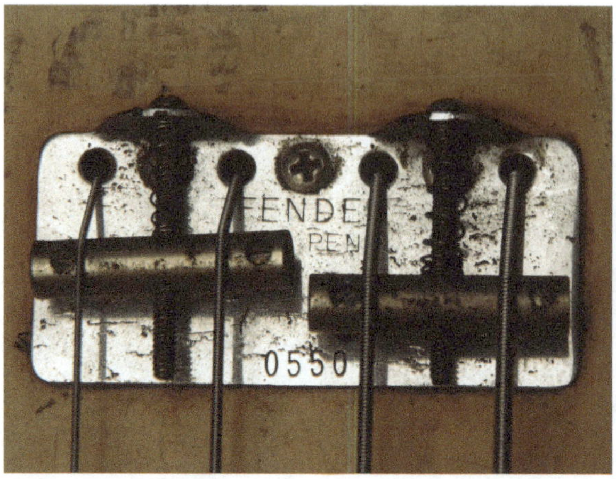

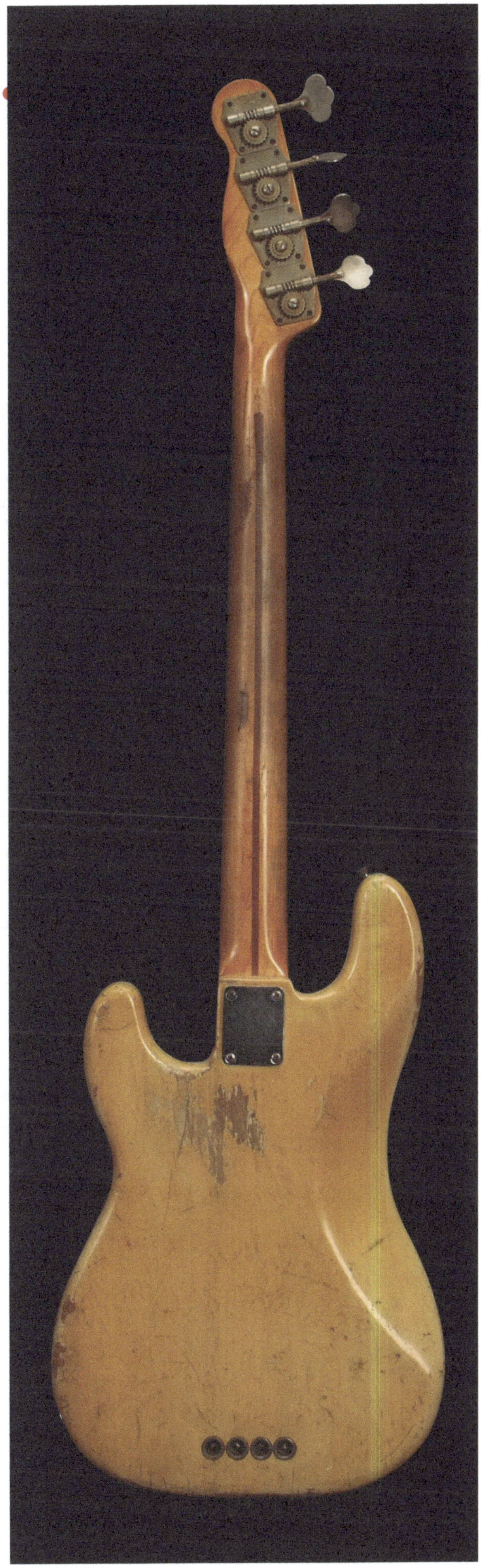

#0667

This '53 bass came from Florida. Someone had added a second single coil pickup and enlarged the control cavity. Also a battery had been added on the backside. It was put back to its original condition, but some traces are still evident.

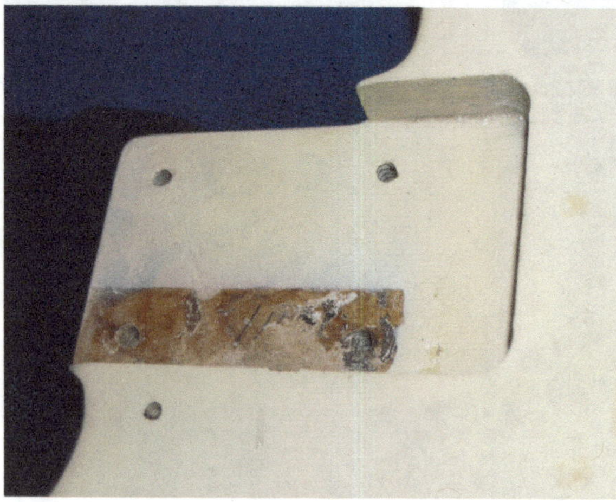

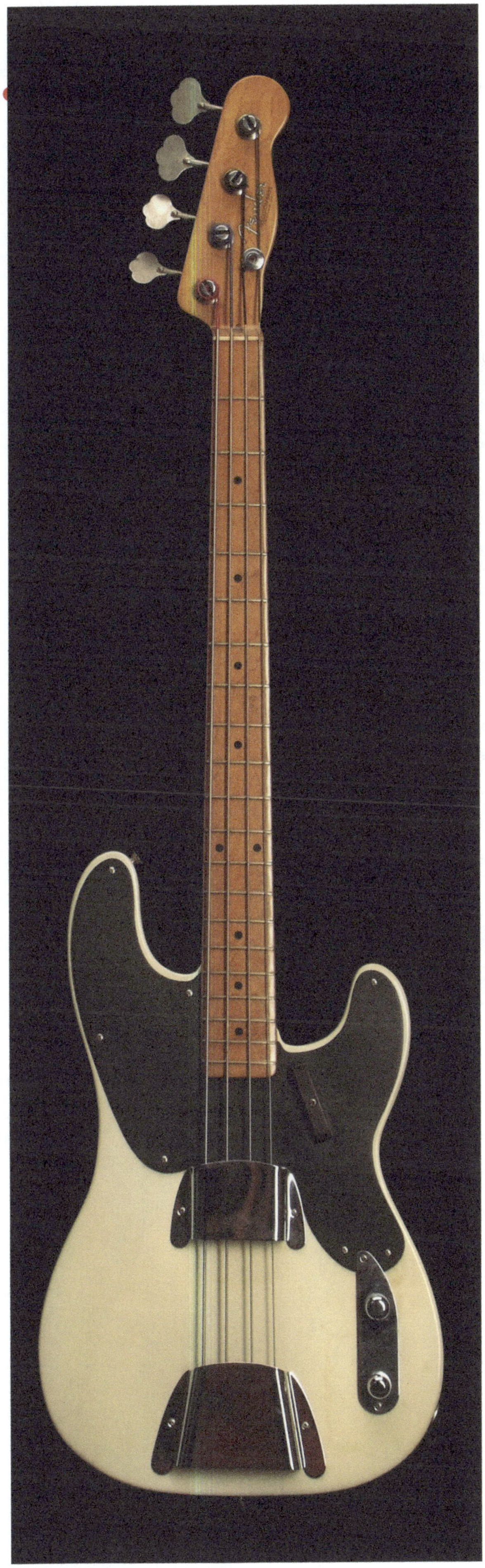

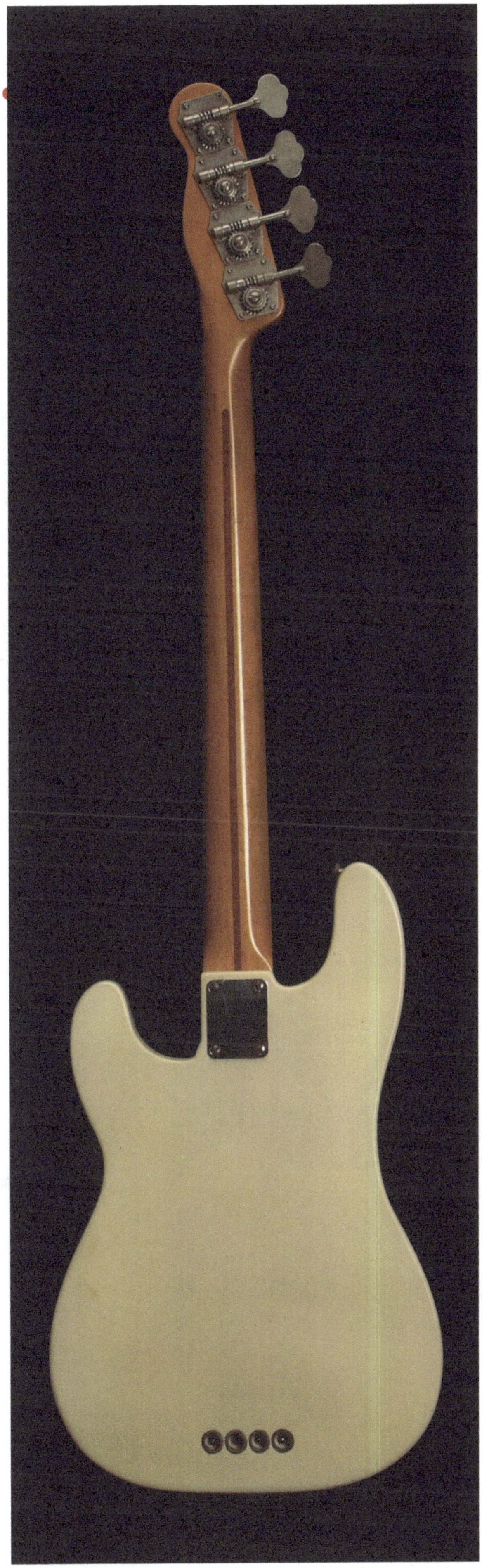

#0672

A Telecaster pickup, a new pickguard and new tuners were added to this bass. Allman Brothers Band bass player Barry Oakley wore a "tie dyed" tee shirt that permanently stained the back of the bass.

The string ferrules look like those on a Telecaster Bass, they are smaller than on original Precision Basses. So the assumption is near that the body also is a Telecaster body.

1953 FENDER PRECISION BASS
PREVIOUSLY OWNED BY BERRY OAKLEY.
BERRY WAS THE ORIGINAL BASS PLAYER
FOR THE ALLMAN BROTHERS BAND

#0685

Another refinished '53 bass. Note the steel saddles that were often preferred by players or just replaced when the phenolic saddles began getting weak. Once routed for a humbucker pickup, it is now back to single coil.

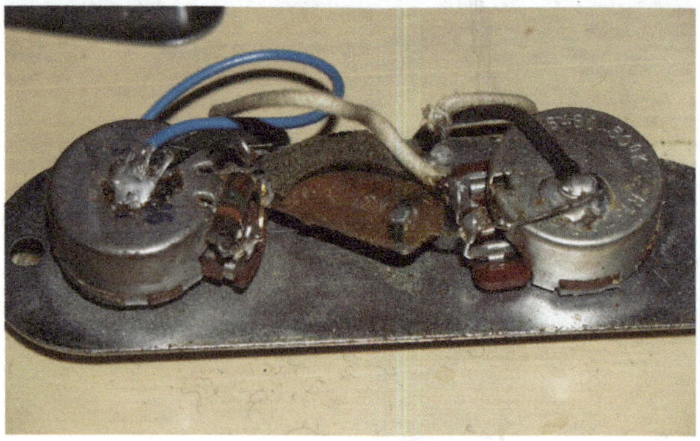

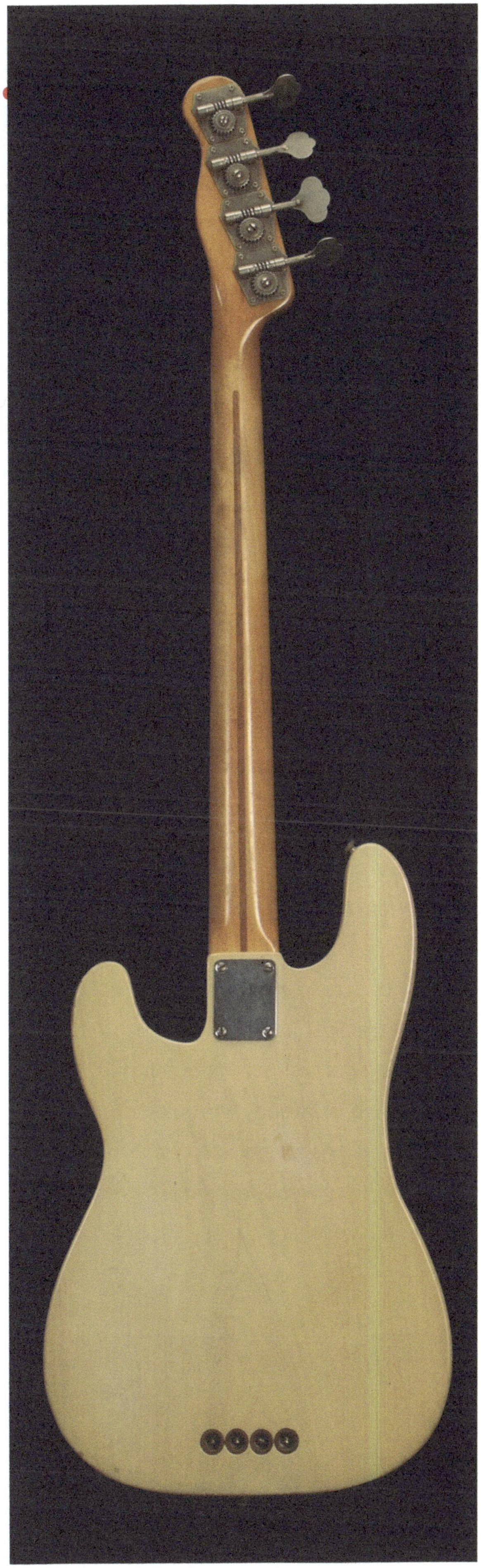

#0691

This bass I bought from my friend Erwin who was a big collector in the 80s. It came with its original gigbag, holding it against my other gigbag, we found out that there were at least two variations of gigbags at that time, one had a more green interior. Erwin made a short holiday trip to bring me the bass and we had lots of fun playing music and hunting for "Apfelstrudel", a traditional German cake that his mother always used to make for him when he was a child.

This might be one of the last slab body basses Fender built before changing over to contoured models. I have never seen a later one. Tadeo only used the short initials TG-3-54, not the exact date anymore.

This corresponds to the masking tape still found in the bass, which says Mary 3-11-54. The body date is 12-53, which means there were three months between body and neck production, indicating they seem to have had enough bodies in storage. Which also means that the sales did not go as well as predicted.

Another interesting feature on this bass is the decal. It is already the later decal where the cloud is positioned very close around the letters. One pot was changed in '93, other than that the bass seems to be in original condition.

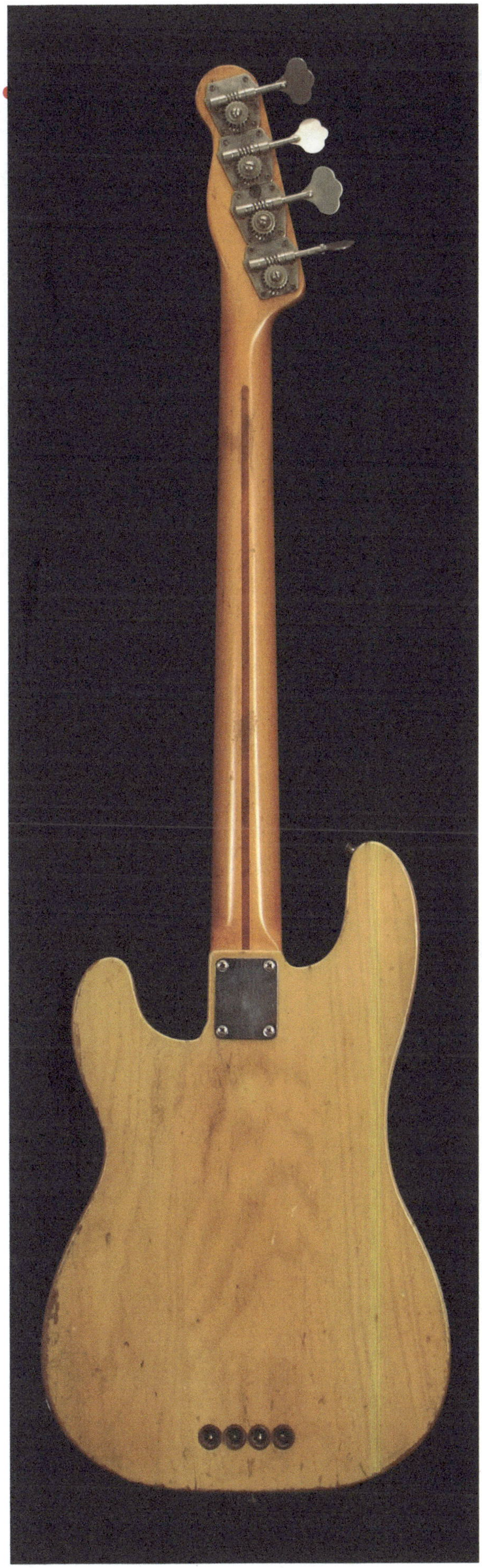

#0691

Note: you can see the environmental influences on lacquer - body, pickguard and neck.

#0747

The typical crack by the E-Tuner. The saddles look like they came from a new Custom Shop Bass. No neckdate or bodydate visible anymore. One of the best sounding basses I have. New pickguard and the bass has been a little routed on the corners.

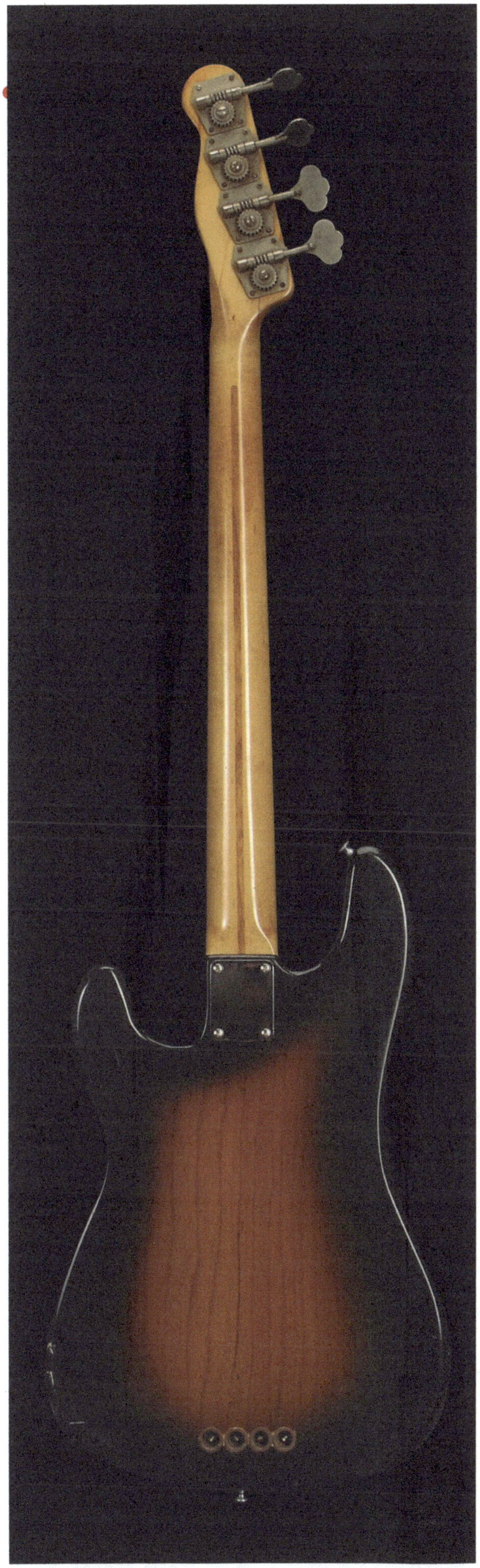

#0772

My friend Mike did this lovely refinishing job. There was just half an inch missing on this bass due to some "woodwork" as the previous owner stated.

By trying to install a different pickguard, we found out that the bass was too small. We decided to bring it back to its original size, and refinish it in black. Here are photos of the restoration process.

#0821

This bass was brought to me at the Great American Guitar Show in Philadelphia. It is heavily routed and refinished. The neck date is TG 2-5-53, the body date was no longer readable.

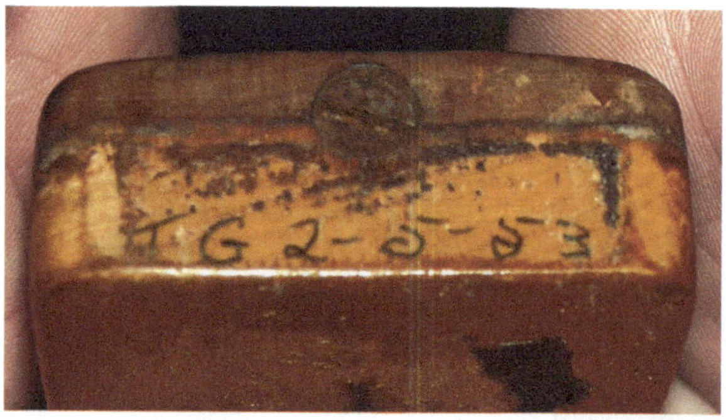

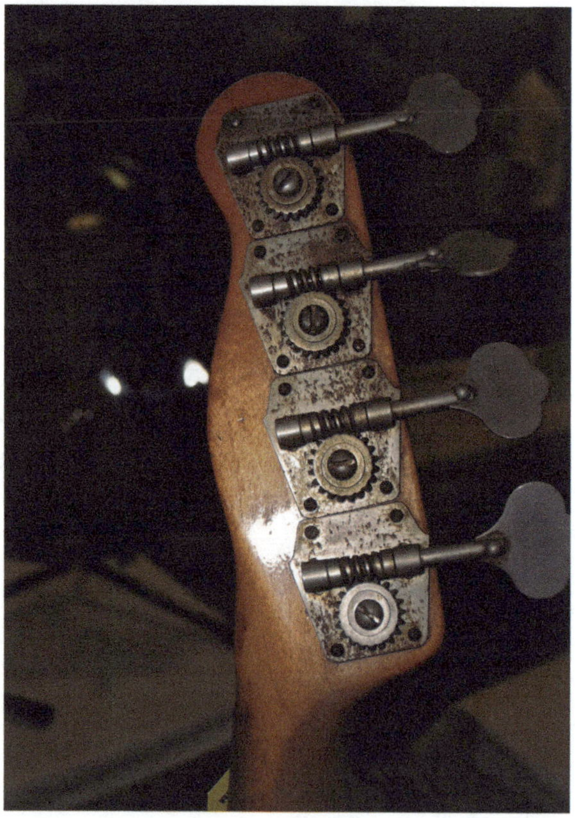

#0834

This 1953 bass belongs to Duke. Neck date 5-27-53, body date 5-11-53 EM. Note the masking tape with "Mary 5-15-53".

The dates are very close together and it would mean, that first the electronics were installed and then later a neck was added, because the neck was not made when the masking tape was signed.

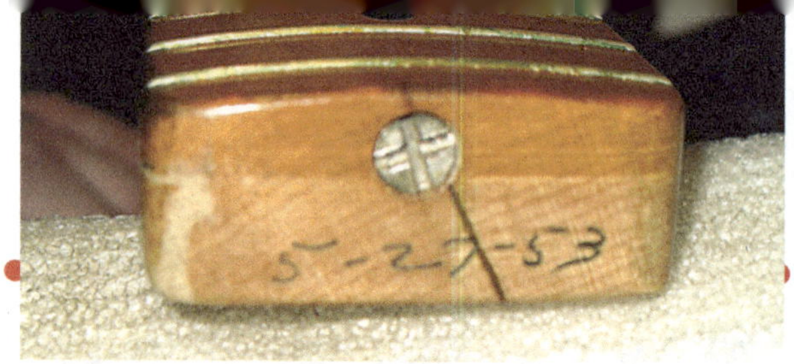

#0836

This bass came from Austin, Texas and is all original except for the pickguard and it has been refinished over the original colour without touching the solder joints. "Paint it Black".

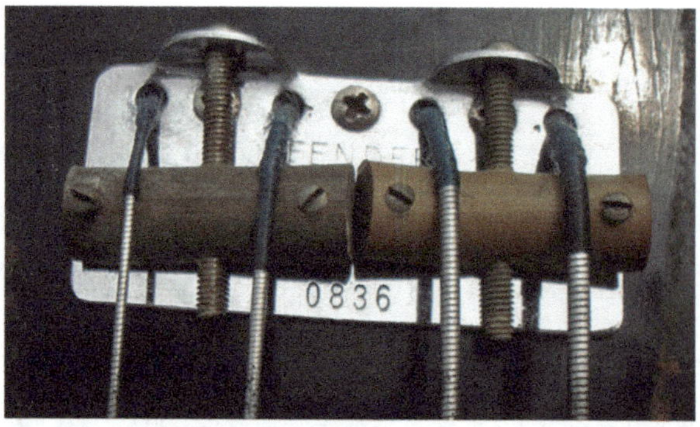

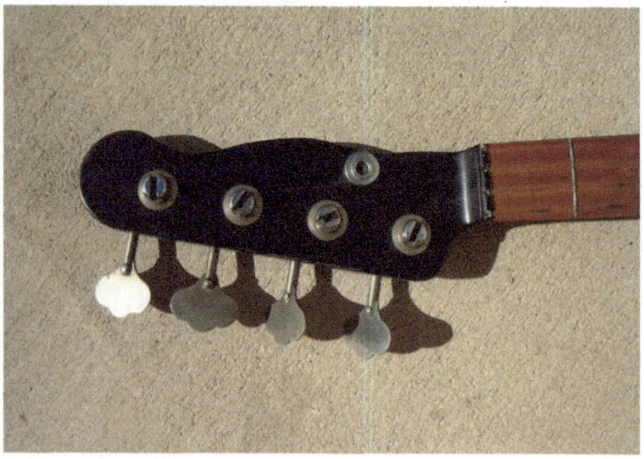

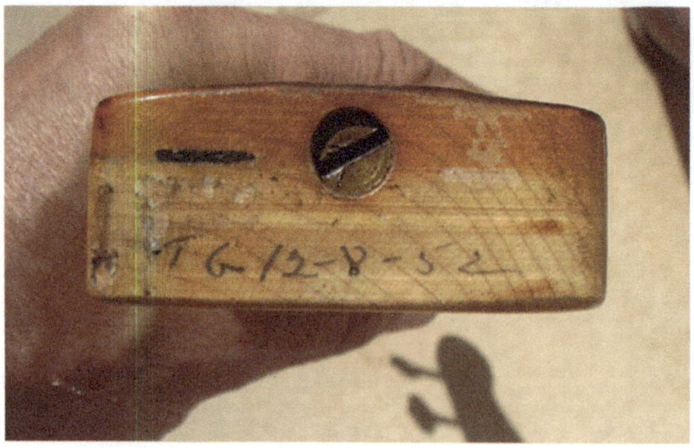

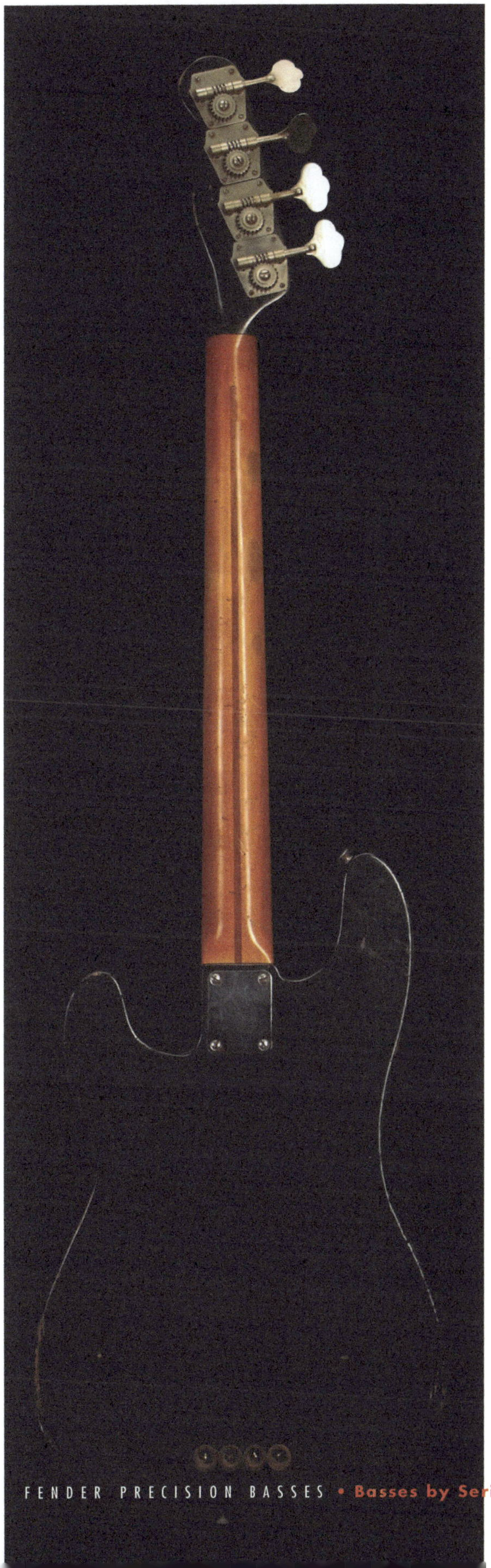

#0917

This bass belongs to Bob Daisley, Sydney, Australia.

He played bass with Stan Webb's band Chicken Shack, Mungo Jerry, Rainbow, Ozzy Osbourne. Bob is also the bassplayer on Gary Moores biggest selling album to date, Charisma/Virgin Records release "Still Got The Blues".

Bob wrote: "I bought it from a friend here in Sydney in 1999 as he needed the money for his wedding/honeymoon. He bought it from Gruhn's in Nashville in the mid 1990s. I have his receipt for $3400, from 1994. I also have a copy of the receipt when it was bought by Penrod Geisinger, the guy in the Impalas, for $35 in 1957. Printed by hand on the body under the neck mounting is EM 3-12-53 (12th March, 1953). The name 'Bush' is burned on the body under the neck plate. The number on the bridge plate is - 'Fender Pat. Pending 0917. I can't see any other serial number anywhere. It has the original strap that came with it in 1953 also. The signature on it is Noel Redding's from the Jimi Hendrix Experience. Noel was actually in Gruhn's shop when my friend was buying it so he got Noel to sign it."

Ione Lambert, Leo Fender & Tadeo Gomez - Leo's Birthday - 1953

Most of the people that worked in the Fender Factory in 1949
Back Row: Bob Fullerton, Don Kroener, Lyle Burke, George Fullerton, Louis Lugar, Cecil Shawbell; Front Row: Fred Fullerton, Lawrence Norberg, Lupe Lopez, Lydia Sanchez, Vangie Ortega and Unidentified man.

#0936

Neck date: 7-30-53, Body date: Bill 2-10-53. Old light overspray on neck and headstock, now mostly worn out, original decal. Changed saddles and pots, otherwise all original parts and finish. This bass belongs to Nacho.

Donald Dunn >

Booker T and the M.G.s was founded by Steve Cropper and Booker T. Jones in 1962. The original bassist, on early hits such as "Green Onions", was Lewie Steinberg; Dunn replaced him in 1965.

This photo shows Dunn with a contoured second version Precision Bass. On his homepage, Dunn states that he bought his first Fender Precision with a maple neck in 58 and still has it.

Booker T and the M.G.s

#0948

This bass came out of Madison, WI. It belonged to a polka player. I was bidding on this bass, was outbid, but my bid helped him a lot. I emailed him: "You owe me a beer when I am in Madison the next time." We finally met a year later and he paid for all my drinks.

Bob Manners

bass player of the Liberace Orchestra, also was an early Fender endorser, here shown with a contoured bass and a later "Narrow Panel" Bassman amp.

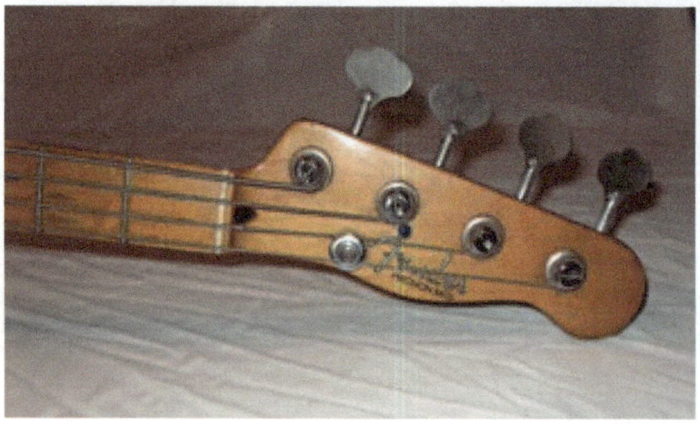

Gene Vincent and The Blue Caps were early Fender endorsers, here shown with a contoured bass, easy to recognize by the white pickguard.

#1070

#1070, where I only had the bridge and the tuners. Now its back alive again, especially custom made for me by a luthier. Body is a one piece swamp ash and neck is an exact copy of my 52 neck. The best thing is, it sounds very good too.

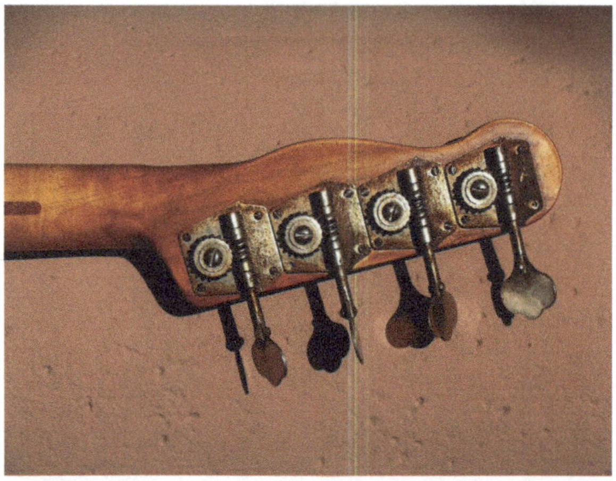

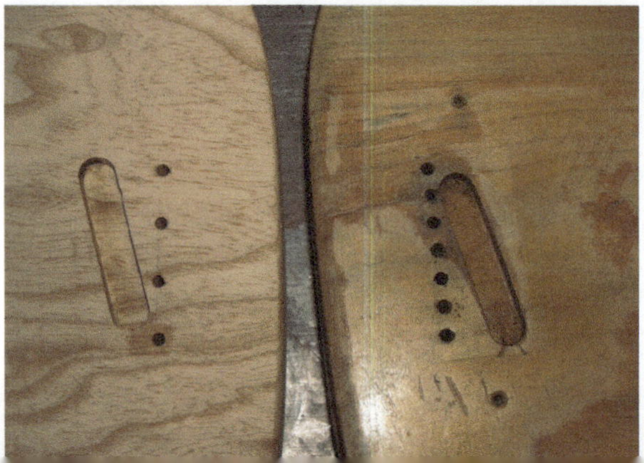

#1088

This 53 P-Bass belongs to Gary. It has one of the nicest weather checkings I have seen. This is exactly how a 53 Precision should look. It has the typical crack at the E-string tuner, nothing serious when repaired. The body marking says Eddie, 3-25-53.

The neck date reads 7-30-53, which would mean that there was a 4 month gap between neck and body production. Note the colour difference between the area under the pickguard and the rest of the body.

"I found her for sale at the Killeen Texas Guitar Center. I dealt with Brett Johnson the store manager who was very helpful in making the deal. In talking to store employees during the buying process, I learned this bass was brought to the store with the leather bag, by a local church member who had tried to sell it at the annual church flea market fund raiser. The church had asked members to bring items, and a member found this in his attic. He brought it in to sell, when no one bought it, they offered it to the Guitar Center. It appears the homeowner had no idea the bass was in his attic. It was up there when he bought the house. "

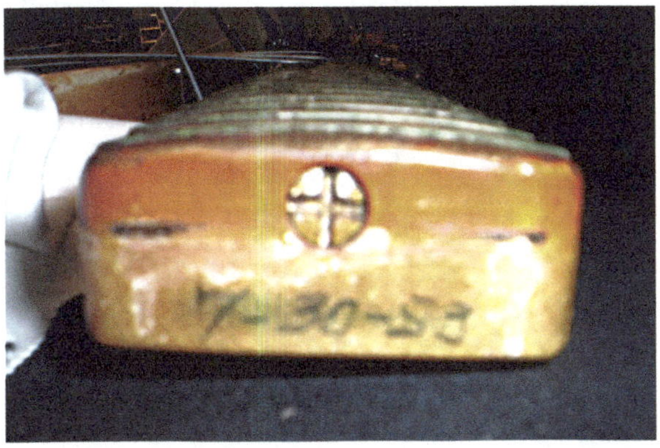

#1119

This 53 P-bass belongs to Duke. It has been stripped but has all original parts except the fibre saddles which were changed to metal saddles, as on many basses. Duke made some sound samples, the sound differences between the metal saddles and the copies of phenolic saddles that I had machined were not that big. RS Guitarworks did a lovely refinishing job on this bass.

Body date is hard to read: -53 Eddie
Neck date: 7-27-53

#1394

This 54 Precision Bass belongs to my friend Ken. Note the very sharp contour for the right arm, this can also be seen on bass #1433, that has be produced in the same month. Later basses do have a more smooth contour.

Masking tape: Virginia 8-16-54
Neck date: T-G-8-54
Body date: 7/54

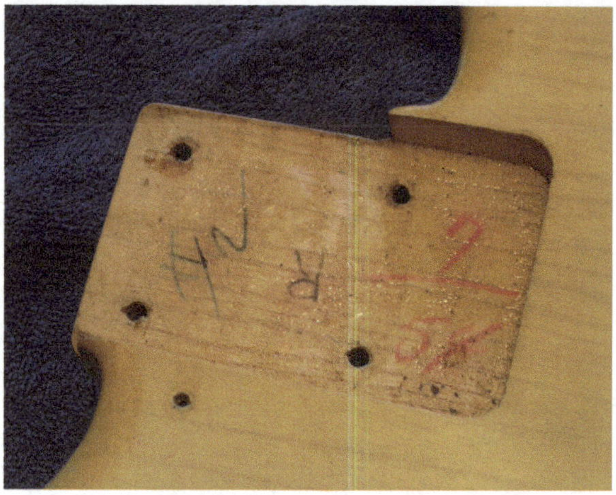

Ken: "The writing under the pickup cover says "Fender Precision SR 0272 1-28-52" - I bought this cover only from an old Fender repairman who had taken it off another (Red!) bass and penciled in the particulars."

Now I know where the pickup cover of my #0272 ended up.

Ken: "Incredible coincidence?! The repairman was a guy name "Red" Rhodes, also a session musician and steel guitar player. He

had a repair shop in North Hollywood, CA, many years ago. He told me that a bass player had come to him with a red bass and was determined to have a humbucking pickup installed. Red tried to convince him otherwise then reluctantly took the job and saved the cover and the pickup. I only bought the cover from him."

#1406

This bass came out of a real estate sale on the south side of Chicago. There must have been a fire somewhere in its life, otherwise it was played and played and played.

High serial number but produced in '52.

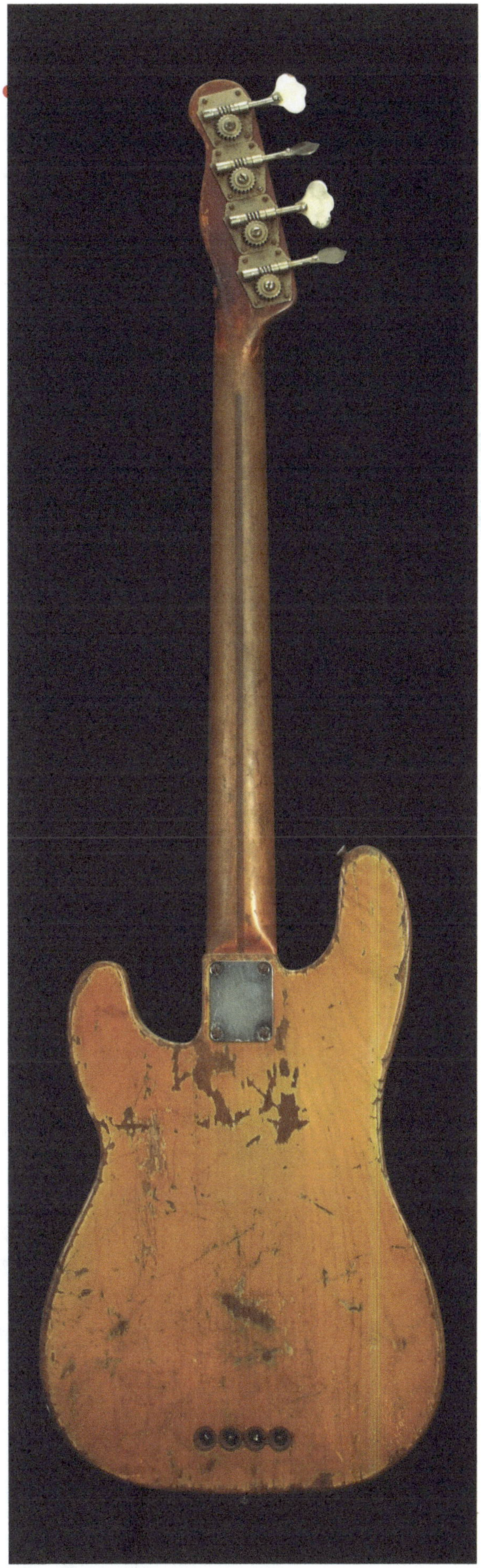

#1433

Note the number of the series #3 in the neck pocket and the body date 7/54. This must be one of the first contoured basses produced in 1954. Stripped and really worn on the backside. New pickup and new pickguard.

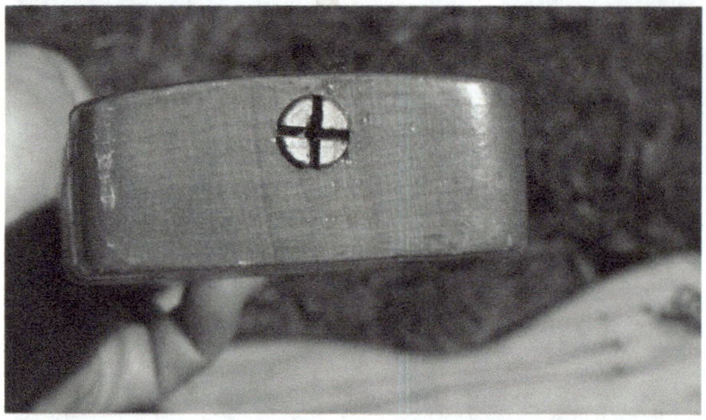

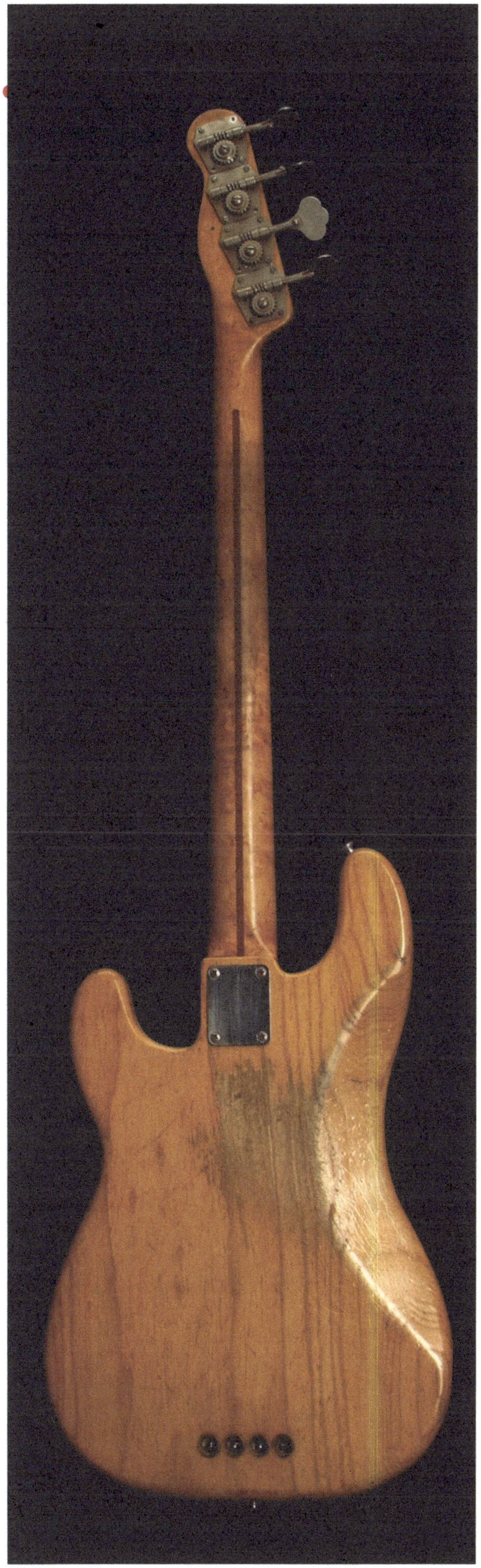

#1443

This 53 P-Bass came from Arlington, Texas. It is original to the last screw. Very well played neck and warped pickguard.

Neck Date: 07-28-53. Body Cavity Date is marked: Eddie 03-24-53.

Original advertisement words:

"This bass was flown into Arlington Guitar Center from the Hollywood, California Guitar Center for me to make an offer on in 1998. I managed to get a good deal on this at the time. It came with the original brown leather gig bag."

Note the second version of the decal, the cloud goes directly around the letters.

Note the extra resistor on the volume pot. Seems to be factory work.

The cutting of the string ferrules was not done by machines as you can easily see.

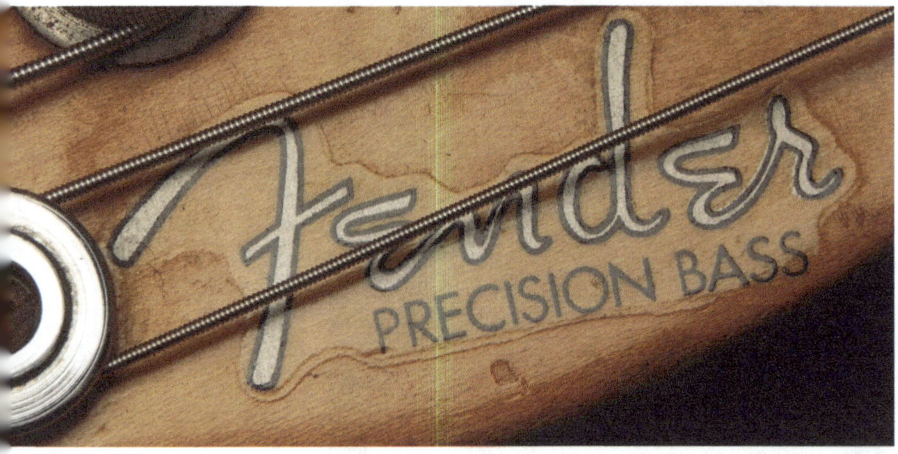

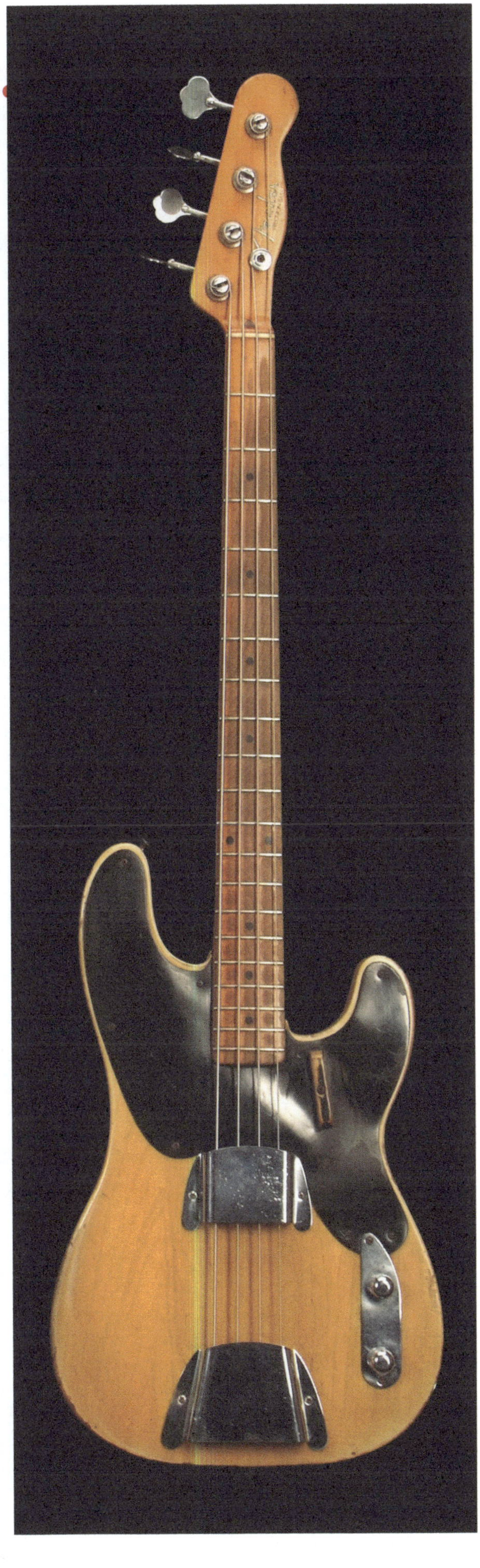

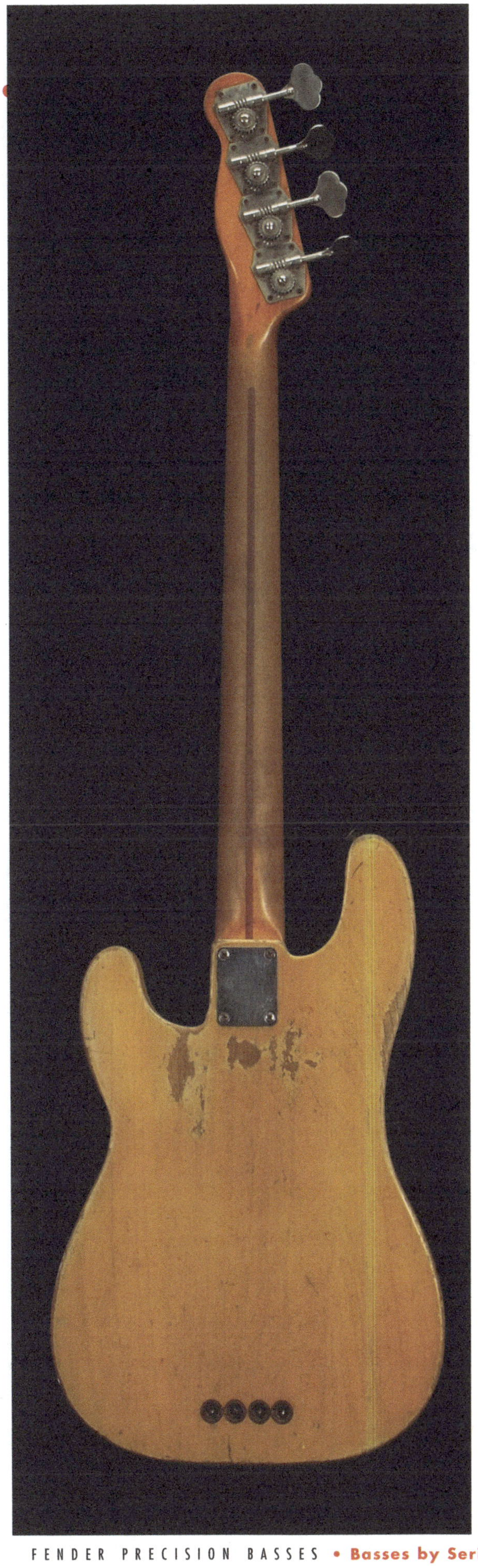

#xxxA

This bass came from Texas and belonged to Bill. Seems like a lot of these basses were sold in Texas in the early 1950s through a shop named McCord in Dallas.

Fred McCord (owner of McCord Music Company) was close friends with Leo Fender. McCords was the premiere Fender dealer outside of California and the place musicians came for all of the latest electric guitar gear.

Bill Black (1926-1965)

Black played bass ('slapped/rockabilly' upright double) with guitarist Scotty Moore, while Elvis Presley played rhythm guitar and sang. During April 1957 sessions recording songs for "Jailhouse Rock", released in September of 1957, Black played a Fender Electric bass.

In 1959 he joined a Memphis group that evolved into Bill Black's Combo. Hi Records released their instrumental "Smokie" in December 1959. "Smokie, Part 2" made the Top 20 in the Billboard Hot 100 chart.

#xxxB

These photos were given to me by Dan Yablonka. The bridge was changed, so the serial number is unknown. The bass has been refinished a long time ago and a new pickguard was added. No neck or body date are visible, pots are changed, so it is hard to determine the exact age of this bass.
www.danyablonka.com

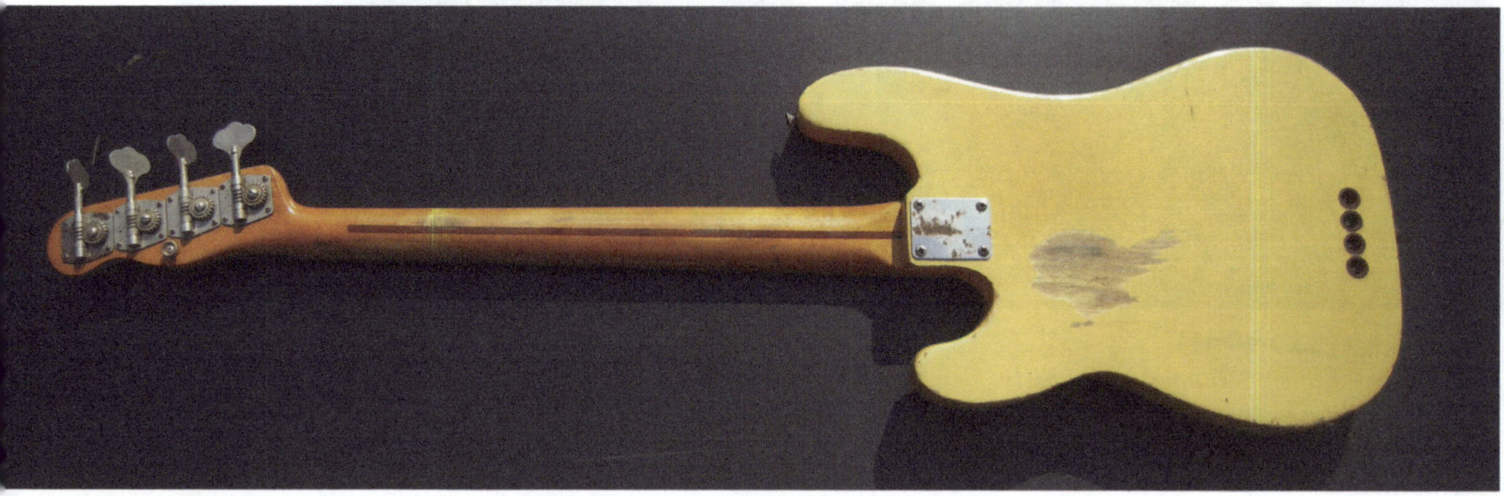

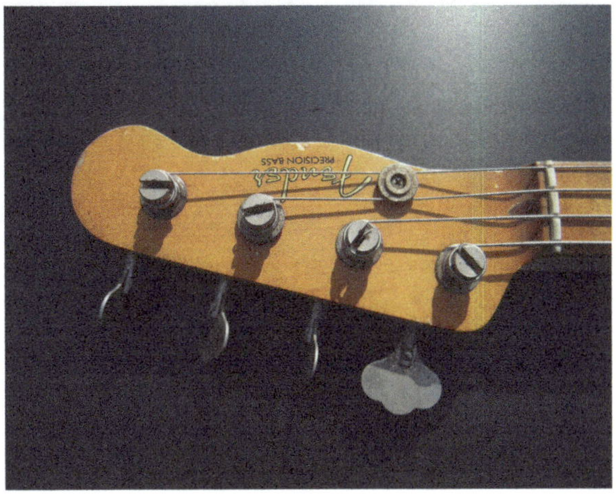

#xxxC

This bass has no serial number because a new bridge was installed. It was sold in Florida by my friend Woody.

Note the D-stamp and the neckdate 11-20-51 and the bodydate 10-30-51. Only 20 days were between the production, in those early days the time gaps were not so big.

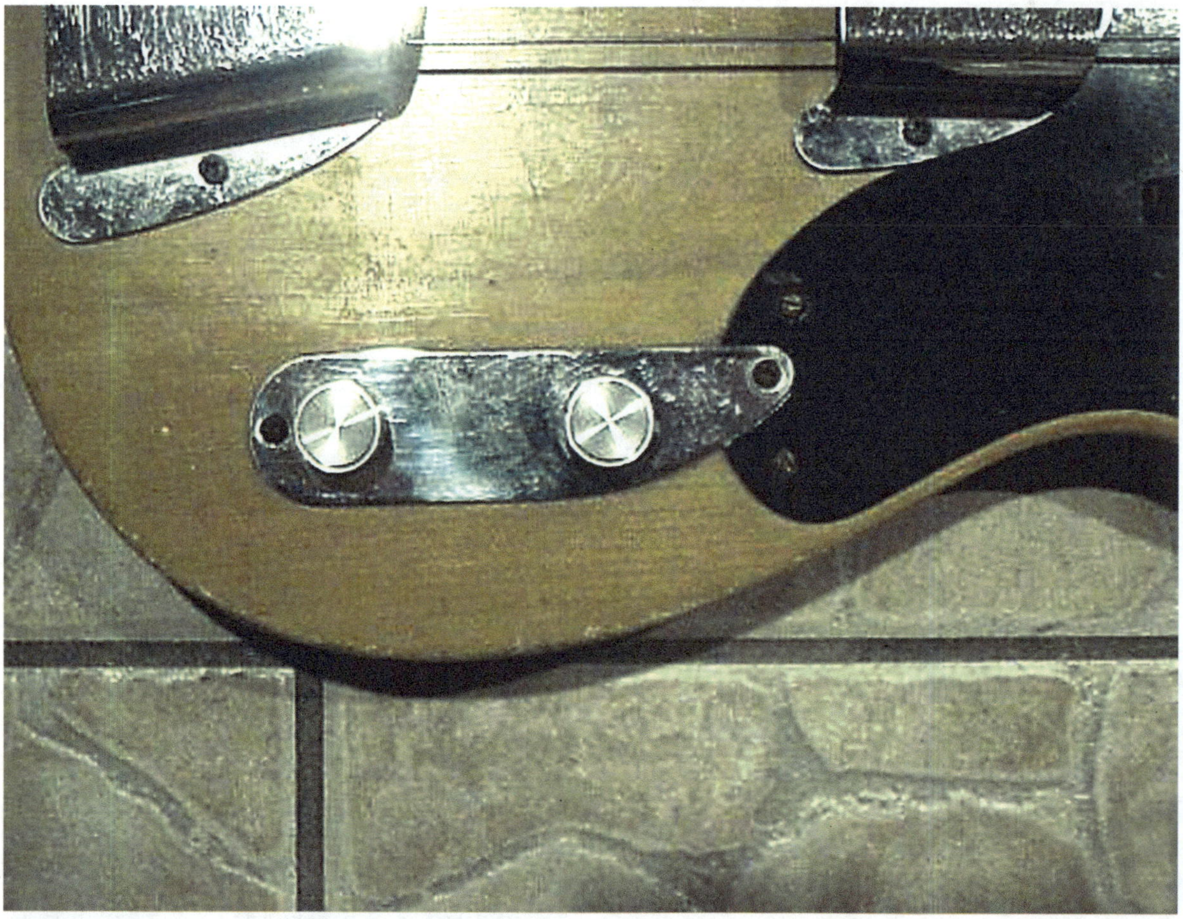

TG 11/20/51 D

Fender
PRECISION BASS

#127

This bass belonged to Clive who has a huge knowledge about old Fender basses. This is the only bass with a 3 digit serial number that I have seen. There are only a few basses reported in the Werner list (79, 161,163, 299, 313, 357, 592, 619). But it is possible that people reported a #0079 as a #79. So I always doubted the existence of these serial numbers until I had seen the number on Clive's bass. This is a 1953 bass. All the other basses Werner has listed date '51 or '52.

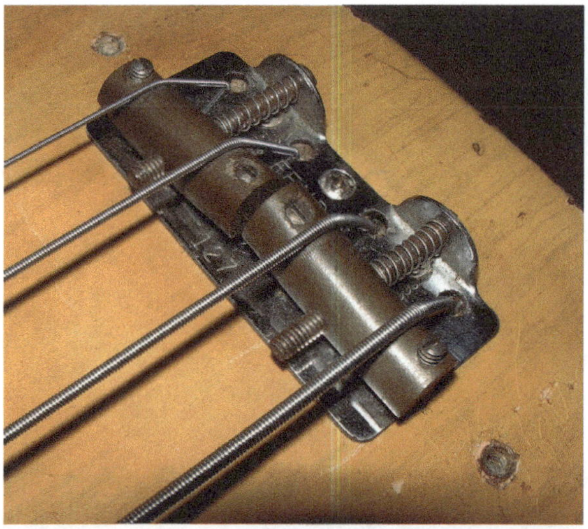

12-8-52

These photos show a 53 Bassman amp, basses #0396 and #1406 and a 54 Bass case.

< Pumpkins and Basses. Indian summer impressions from Wisconsin.

American icons

$3.00

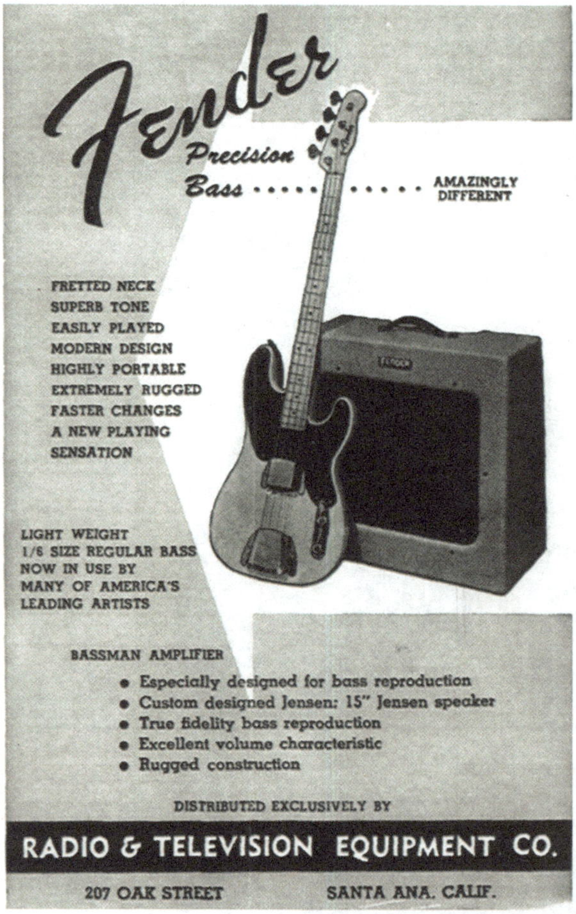

Shifty Henry

John Willie "Shifty" Henry (1921-1958), was known as a double bass and bass guitar player, and blues songwriter and was in demand as a session musician and arranger in Los Angeles, California in the 1940s and 1950s.

Henry recorded with and arranged for the elite of jazz and rhythm and blues, including Dinah Washington, Dizzy Gillespie, Charles Mingus, The Treniers and Miles Davis. He also played in the house band for the Dean Martin and Jerry Lewis television show.

His name is mentioned in a verse of "Jailhouse Rock" by Jerry Leiber and Mike Stoller: "Shifty Henry said to Bugs, for heaven's sake, no one's looking, now's a chance to make a break."

Henry was selected by Leo Fender to receive an early electric Fender Precision Bass.

(1953) Early fifties advertisement for Fenders first electric bass Fender Precision - Instruments get out of date too

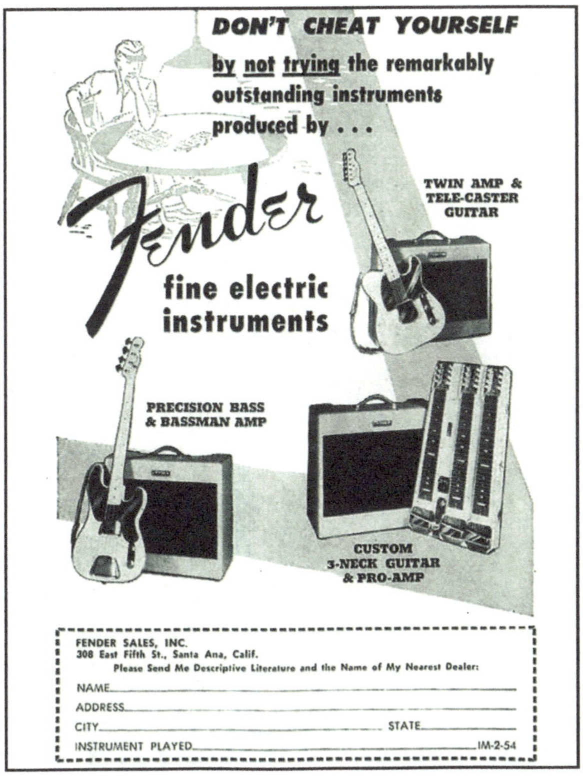

Fender Precision - Don't cheat yourself Early Fender advertisement featuring the Precision bass and Telecaster guitar

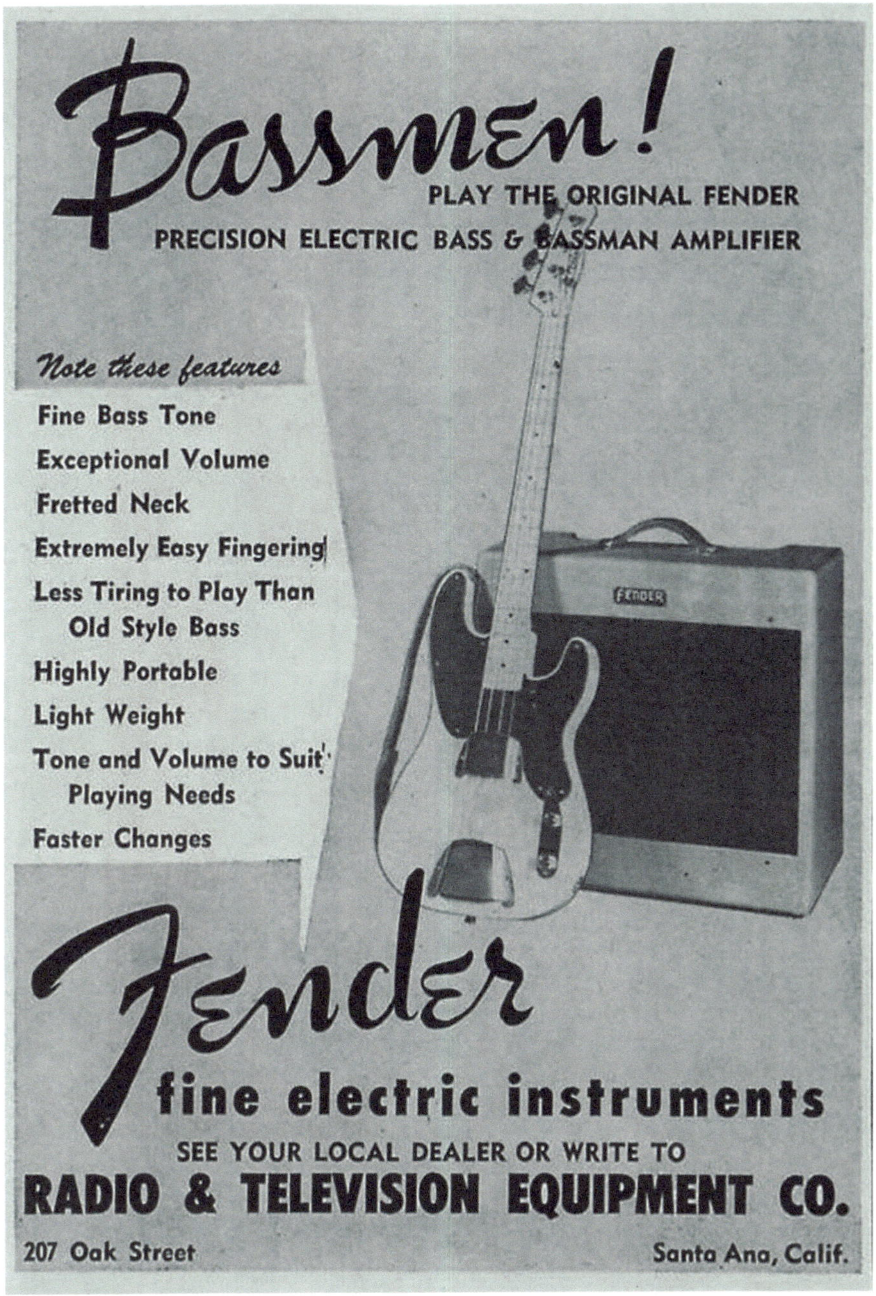

Fender advertisement (1953) underlining the modern features of the Fender Precision bass, and bassman amplifier

PRECISION BASS

The new four string Precision Bass is one of the most revolutionary instruments to make an appearance in many years. It is the answer to every bass player's desire for a portable instrument of extremely fine tone quality, plus playing ease and comfort. This remarkable new instrument is infinitely easier to play than a conventional bass, inasmuch as the technique is like that used in playing a guitar. Very little string action is required to obtain full rich bass volume, thereby eliminating the effort that went in to playing the old style bass.

The neck of this instrument is slender and fretted, and the string adjustment is close to the frets, thus enabling the player to play with greatly increased speed. Most players find that their technique improves very rapidly with the use of this new instrument and that they can play considerably more difficult work than ever before.

With the Precision Bass it is possible to obtain considerably more volume than with a conventional instrument. The space required for storage or carrying of this instrument is approximately ⅙ of that required for the old type bass.

The Fender Precision Bass opens an entirely new field of bass playing, and already they have become stock items in a great many of the nation's top musical organizations.

Available as an accessory is a fine molded plush lined case, covered in Dupont "Grain Hair Seal," or a padded plastic leather bag.

LIONEL HAMPTON

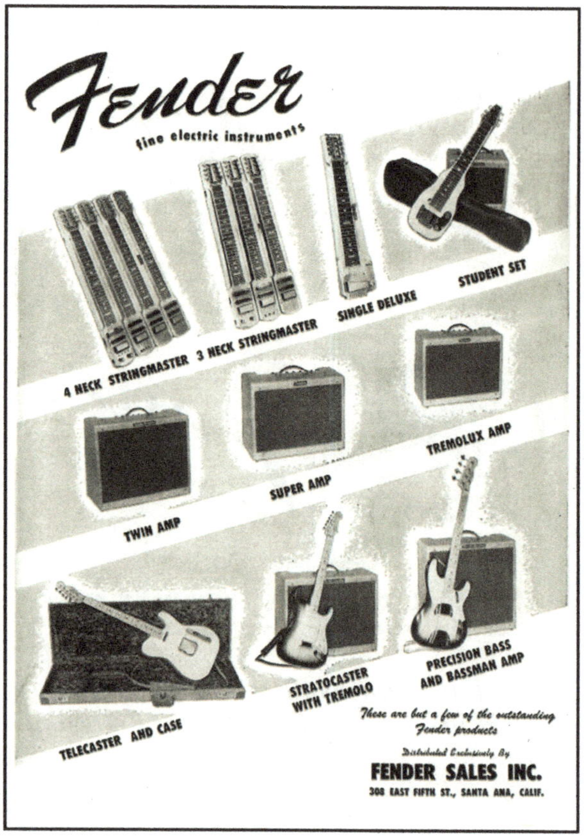

Fender fine electric instruments 1955
Early Fender advertisement for the Telecaster and Stratocaster guitars, Precision bass, and Twin, Super, and Tremolux amplifiers

Louis Jordan (1908 – 1975) was an American rhythm & blues musician, songwriter and bandleader who enjoyed his greatest popularity from the late 1930s to the early 1950s. Known as "The King of the Jukebox", Jordan released dozens of hit songs, including "Saturday Night Fish Fry" and the multi-million seller "Choo Choo Ch'Boogie. One of his biggest hits was "Caldonia".

Fender Fine Electric Instruments

PRECISION BASS and BASSMAN AMP

Amp Size:
Height .... 23"
Width .... 22½"
Depth .... 10½"

PRECISION BASS

One of the greatest of modern instrument developments. Fast becoming the favorite of musicians in every field. Compact in size, but very large in performance. Requires only a fraction of the effort to play as compared to old style accoustic basses. Extremely well suited for that fast delicate playing technique. When used with proper amplifier, it will produce considerably more volume than old style basses. The tone leaves nothing to be desired and the portability is the answer to every bass player's dream.

BASSMAN AMP

The unparalleled performance of this amplifier is readily recognized by all qualified listeners.

Provides true bass amplification or may also be used for other instruments due to its widely varying tonal characteristics.

Heavy duty solid wood cabinet covered with diagonal, brown and white stripe airplane luggage linen. Chrome plated chassis, on-and-off switch, ground switch, standby switch, bass, treble and presence tone controls, two volume controls, two input jacks, four 10" heavy duty Jensen speakers, 50 Watts output.

FOR FURTHER INFORMATION, SEE YOUR LOCAL MUSIC DEALER, OR WRITE:

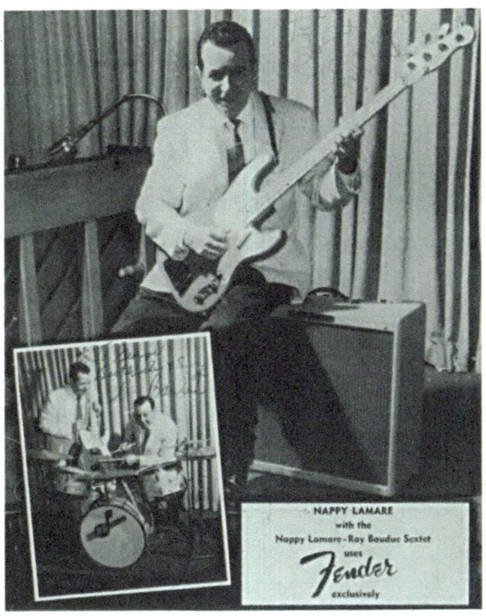

Nappy Lamare (1905 - 1988)

was an American jazz banjoist, guitarist and vocalist, perhaps best-known for his work with the Bob Crosby band in the early 1940s. In 1947 he became a partial owner of a club in Los Angeles called '47'. Later on, he formed a band called the "Riverboat Dandies." The band recorded two albums for Capitol, Riverboat Dandies and Two Beat Generation. It was during the time with the Riverboat Dandies when Lamare began playing a four-string Fender bass instead of the banjo, due to an injury to his left hand.

Freddie Bell and the Bellboys

Freddie Bell and the Bellboys were an American vocal group, influential in the development of rock and roll in the 1950s. In 1955, they made their first recordings including a cover version of Leiber and Stoller's "Hound Dog" (first recorded by Big Mama Thornton).

They were offered a part in "Rock Around the Clock", the first rock and roll movie, starring Bill Haley. The first single for their new label Mercury, "Giddy Up A Ding Dong", was featured in the film.

PAY LESS AT
ERRY LEE LEW
MUSIC TRUCK
RECORDS AT WHOLESALE... OR NEAR

Gene Vincent and The Blue Caps

The Treniers

The Treniers were an American musical group led by twins Cliff and Claude Trenier, which included Shifty Henry and later James (Jimmy) Johnson on bass. One of the first times rock and roll appeared on national television was in May 1954 when the Treniers appeared on the "Colgate Comedy Hour" hosted by Dean Martin and Jerry Lewis. This can be found amongst other clips on "YouTube". The group appeared in several films in the 1950s including "The Girl Can't Help It" and "Don't Knock the Rock" (which also featured Haley).

TRENIERS

52 Bassman (TV-Front)

53 Bassman (Wide Panel)

53 Bassman (Wide Panel)

In 1951 the Precision Basses were offered with a Pro Amp, in '52 with a "TV"-Bassman, from '53 on with the "Wide Panel"-Bassman amp. Note the serial number "0458" and the original cover.

Special Thanks

Special thanks to George Edmonston Jr. for letting me use the wonderful "History of the Development and Early Production of the Fender Precision Bass". He put together all the information that is available in other books in just a great way. Filling it up with the photos was great fun. The story is a perfect match with the rest of the book.

Also special thanks have to go to Dave Wallis, not only for the photos but for sharing his opinions and his help in the final days of the production of this book.

Also Roger Brant from Canada was a great help in proof-reading most parts of this book.

If there are any mistakes left, they are my fault, cause I changed things later again.

I would like to thank my publisher Ron Middlebrook for the support and help during this project. I also would like to thank my designer Jürgen Wüst for the fun time.

Besides, the Fender Discussion Page, **www.fenderforum.com** is a great page with a lot of knowledgeable members.

If you have any new (old) basses, pictures, more information, or questions, contact me: Bass52@gmx.de

Detlef Schmidt (Germany)
March 2010

Credits:
All photos by the author and the bass owners that are noted on the pages, except:

Centerstream Publishing: pages 9, 10, 11, 22, 24, 25, 109, 112, 113, 148, 149, 150, 151
Michael: pages 32 and 33
Irene and Don: pages 46, 47, 48, 49
Mabron McKinney: page 62
Loren L. Ross: page 85
Getty Images: pages 111, 129, 152, 153, 154, 155, 156, 157